LIFE'S LONG JOURNEY

10 Practical Lessons for Living
a Successful, Positive Life — Everyday

NING JULIAN SAMSON

iUniverse, Inc.

New York Lincoln Shanghai

Life's Long Journey
10 Practical Lessons for Living a Successful, Positive Life—Everyday

Copyright © 2006 by Ning

iUniverse books may be ordered through booksellers or by contacting:

iUniverse
2021 Pine Lake Road, Suite 100
Lincoln, NE 68512
www.iuniverse.com
1-800-Authors (1-800-288-4677)

ISBN-13: 978-0-595-39970-3 (pbk)
ISBN-13: 978-0-595-86126-2 (cloth)
ISBN-13: 978-0-595-84358-9 (ebk)
ISBN-10: 0-595-39970-3 (pbk)
ISBN-10: 0-595-86126-1 (cloth)
ISBN-10: 0-595-84358-1 (ebk)

Printed in the United States of America

With God's love in my heart, I seek to live life with love, peace, joy, happiness, and contentment. I hope that my story of survival will encourage every woman, man, and child who is facing a crisis to keep embracing a life of love, faith and hope for tomorrow. We must continue to live and enjoy each moment of the day with patience and perseverance, for we are all living on borrowed time. We each must learn from our own Life's Long Journey and we must continue to reap life's rewards. In other words—celebrate life!

I dedicate this book to my beloved mother, Agripina Samson.

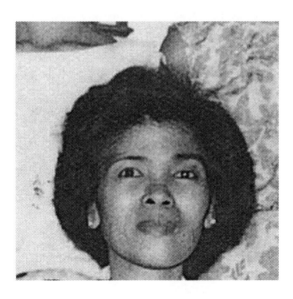

Ning's mother

CONTENTS

Chapter 7   Life in America.............................**123**
Lesson Seven: Be grateful for all that life has to offer.

Chapter 8   A Teacher's Dream...........................**154**
Lesson Eight: You will become what you believe.

ACKNOWLEDGMENT

I am deeply grateful to my mother, who showed me the way to live positively in today's fast world; to my father, who showed me the importance of giving and forgiving; to my three children, Maria, Juliann and Edward, my joy and my inspiration; to my whole family, who showed me their unconditional love while going through my challenges; to my best friend, Lucille and Ollie King; who were always available during all my trials; to Liisa Rahkonen—without her, I would have not started writing this book; to my friend Carol Ball, whose talents in photography and paintings inspired me to paint my mother, whom I use as the cover of this book; to Father Steckler of Saint Anthony Parish Church of Waldport, Oregon, who gave me a lot of spiritual motivation while writing this book; to Joy Moran, who helped me in editing; and to all my friends, teachers, colleagues and neighbors all over the world, who continuously supports me through my journey.

Most of all, I thank God for the precious gift of life, which I gratefully accept.

Our Family Picture. From Left Standing—*Ate* Linda, eldest; Ning, second child; Lina, fourth child; Tino, third child; Sitting from Left—Mom, Agripina; Dad, Francisco; Front from Left—Tessie, fifth child; Shirley, youngest, daughter; Francisco Jr, youngest son

INTRODUCTION

I have written this book just for you, my readers, so that I may share all that I have learned and experienced in my life—success, failure, faith, hope, and love. I'd also like to describe some of the people I have come to know. Writing this book has fulfilled my longtime promise to tell my story, hoping someday, maybe, that you, too, will have your own life story to pass on.

Two years ago, while having a cup of tea at my friend Liisa's kitchen table, she handed me a term project about her spiritual beliefs. I was so fascinated by her story that, during the course of our conversation, I told her part of my life story. She commented, in a very determined voice, that my story should be told to others, too. I didn't pay much attention to her suggestion at first, and I continued reading her manuscript. A week later, she showed me her written version of what I had told her. As I read through the lines, both of us started crying. I went home and thought about it all night.

The next morning, still thinking about writing a book, and watching the powerful waves of the Pacific Ocean from my front window, I asked myself why not. I enjoy reading. I surround myself with a gazillion books. Being a teacher, I have valued and evaluated books all my life. I have written numerous manuals and insurmountable curricula for my classes and seminars. I thought all that should make writing a book easy.

Suddenly fear settled in and I started doubting my abilities. Yes, I had accomplished all of the above, but, no, I had *never* written and published a book. I know the devil tried to talk me out of it, but my angel told me to do it. I decided that I could at least *try*.

I knew that it was time for me to go to the next level. To reach this level, I had to believe in myself and put myself to the test. Three problems came to mind: First, the English language was a barrier. I am a foreign-born U.S. citizen, and English does not come easy to me. I speak and write in unrefined English. I told myself that maybe this plan to write was not a good idea. Maybe my friends were suggesting it just to make me feel good. Because of the monumental work to be done, I almost gave up. But then I figured, if *He* wants me to write my story, *He* will see me through. That settled that. The second problem was that I could write technical manuals and procedures, but to write a descriptive, vivid picture of an event was still a big challenge. In school, when my business teacher told us that business letters must be short, concise, and to the point, then I thought I had died and gone to heaven. Maybe that was why I took business and not English.

When I started writing, I began to read books about publishing and autobiographies. I began to admire authors who could write and publish five books in a year, while it had taken me two and a half years just to submit my manuscript, and the publisher would want more. This was the third problem—how can my idea become a manuscript and eventually end up on a bookstore shelf?

So who am I to write this book? I am not a writer; I am a teacher. Teaching comes naturally for me. It's my gift, just like my mother has said. As a teacher, I've always cherished the moments when I have seen my students succeed. As a writer, I want to inspire the readers of my stories. I know that it is going to take a long time to reach a wide audience. I wanted a book that would touch the hearts of my readers. To accomplish that goal, I had to read, read, read and write, write, write. It was not easy. It took dedication, hard work, patience, and a lot of long hours, burning the midnight candles—just like I used to do, growing up.

Writing is hard enough, but to write a book about my own life was even harder. I was taking a leap of faith to a level that I knew could be rewarding when it's done with joy and peace. I was excited. I started searching and digging through whatever what was left of the pictures from my childhood and documents of my schooling, writing about funny events in my life that were worth telling, and also reaching out and asking my older sister, *Até* Linda, for some of her recollections. It brought about a lot of good and sad memories. I seriously considered asking my mother, who knows all about me, but I dismissed the idea. I wanted to surprise her. I had planned to dedicate the book to her, so telling her would have defeated my purpose. I wanted it to be a big surprise, especially when she found out that I had painted her on the cover of the book. She would be amazed because she had always wanted me to paint. All my brothers and sisters have drawing talent and are all artistic in their own ways. Instead, I chose to read and study. After this book is published, I would like to go home, back to the Philippines, and be able to hand her the first copy of this book for her birthday or Christmas. Furthermore, upon reading through countless books about the length of time it takes a regular publisher to print a book, I decided to self-publish. My mother is in her eighties and not doing well, so it might be too late if I wait too long.

For a beginner to write a great book takes a lot of planning and preparation. Just like a teacher, planning a lesson is the most important part of teaching. Like a teacher, a writer, must have a goal—simple enough that the reading audience can understand—a book that the world would want to buy, read, and learn from.

I have three purposes for writing about this part of my life:

- To surround you with an impenetrable shield constructed from ten powerful life lessons so you can live a richer life, without worry and fear

- To empower you through my quotes, poems, and lessons

- To sell books and donate part of the proceeds to educate, improve the health of disadvantaged children and make a difference in people's lives

I have learned a lot from life. Growing up in a dark, dreary, crowded crawl space filled with mice, spiders, pigs, and chickens, and seven brothers and sisters in Manila, Philippines, was challenging enough. I was determined, by going to school and finishing college, to help my family get out of extreme poverty. I didn't do it on my own; I was blessed and had some help. I persevered in my studies and was granted several scholarships. I succeeded.

My dream of becoming a teacher came true because of my mother and father's faith in me. Their motivating spirit and spiritual values got me through the toughest fights in my life.

While teaching, I came to know and watch a young man's dream come true through his mother's love and support.

Mary, his mother and I met several times at the University of Washington. He was a determined teenager who, in later years, together with his friend (Paul Allen), revolutionized the computer industry and became the richest man in the world. His name was Bill Gates.

I enjoy teaching. I do not consider my job to be complete unless I know that each of my students has reached his or her goal of finding a job—not just a job, but a rewarding job.

Along with successes come overwhelming hardships. The miracles that I have experienced after suffering from uterine cancer, nearly dying from a car accident, getting divorced, and being homeless, abused, and discriminated against have taught me that life is worth fighting for.

I have learned to enjoy and celebrate life. I also believe that a positive outlook in life can turn a bitter life into a better life.

This is not the end but a beginning of my new-found love— writing. I would love for you, my readers, to read it through, and I hope that you pass it on. I hope that you enjoy reading it as much as I enjoyed writing it—my *life's long journey.*

My Mother's Love

Ning Samson

She gets tired and works hard each night

To put our home in order, clean, healthy and bright.

Her hard life and wrinkles may show all through her face,

Beneath this, her love and true sacrifice shows all of her grace.

She always wears a smile—it shows through her eyes.

She is always around to give me some wise advice.

She gives me the courage, faith and hope to grow

She said, "Your name means a Shining Star. You will some-

day shine and glow."

My mother inspired me to live each moment with joy.

She instilled in me to love God, live life to the fullest, and enjoy

She lends a helping hand even when her life was tough and gray.

To her, this is temporary, patience will pave the way.

My mother's love is genuine—it shows and it shines.

All the kindness she brings; her heart is so divine.

Although she is far away, across the ocean, across the sea,

She is always in my heart—that is where she will always be.

I love you, Mom.

I wrote this poem on the airplane when I left the Philippines

in 1970, thinking that I might not see her again.

Chapter 1

CHALLENGES FROM THE START

Lesson One: Be thankful for what you have, and make the most of what you've got.

Early Childhood

*I*n my neighborhood in Manila, Philippines, desperate survival was commonplace. Looking back, I think that our family had been very fortunate to have a home in a four-and-a-half-foot tall crawl space underneath my aunt and uncle's (Tia' Bennie and Tio' Indong's) house. Their home above us was huge, compared to most houses in our neighborhood. It was filled to capacity with their five children, three other relatives, a house girl, and a cook.

We lived on O'Donnell Street in the congested town of Blumentritt, a district of Santa Cruz, Manila. The crawl space where we lived had been patiently put together by my father, who used only a broken handsaw, a claw hammer, and a lot of scavenged and salvaged materials. He made our home more from good intentions than of sturdy post and lath. We lived in a dark, cramped area that, some thought, was more suitable for a small storage space than for our family. In spite of our living conditions, we gratefully accepted our crawl space as our home. My mother and father thanked my uncle who had given us this space to live. We considered ourselves very fortunate, compared to other families nearby who lived in very crowded cardboard huts. My parents gave prayers of gratitude to God for providing for our family.

The building beside Tia'(Aunt) Bennie and Tio'(Uncle) Indong's house was a two-story cement wall of a molasses factory, which radiated sweet-smelling heat, like a furnace burning in the hot sun. To the left of our crawl space was the neighbor's eight-foot cement wall, which separated their property from ours. To our right was a busy city street where we heard the constant shrill rasp of brakes and honking traffic. We were exposed to the exhaust fumes from hundreds of rapidly moving freight trucks, cars, buses, motor scooters, and jeepneys (salvaged U.S. military jeeps left over during World War II). Our front door opened into a public alley that funneled a continuous flow of foot traffic past our house, day and night.

> The effect of life's problems can either tear you apart like a hurricane or toughen you like a rock.

Across from our house, several families were densely packed into concrete apartment buildings intermingled with shanty huts built of corrugated tin, wooden boards, and plastic tarps. Millions of people lived in and around Manila. Families crowded together into neighborhoods built on unstable piers with recycled wooden boards, corrugated tin and the dwellings spilled far beyond the urban boundaries into the farmland.

In spite of our living conditions, my parents' sincere and creative efforts instilled in us the qualities of love, faith, hope, respect, gratitude, hard work, resourcefulness, thrift, and perseverance. My mother and father taught me, in many ways, lessons that will remain in my heart and my spirit in a very powerful way throughout my life. The lessons I learned from my parents were like the strong currents moving invisibly beneath the ocean floor. Their steady influence strengthened my will to survive among the many challenges of my own life's lessons.

The dirt floor of our home was packed smooth, hard, and shiny as leather, as a result of the constant back and forth traffic from the bare feet of all the members of my large family. My mother constantly swept the dirt floor to keep it clean, tidy, and respectable for all of us.

Father's Resourceful Efforts

Our rent was based on father's meager and scarce salary. He worked as a cargo checker at the pier. His job was to keep an inventory of the international containers of cargo coming in from foreign countries, including the United States. Every day he would rise up early at four in the morning, then take the public transportation called jeepney, then walk a quarter of a mile to his work site, wait for two hours every day for his name to be called to work, just to find out sometimes that his name was not on the list to work that day. He was a very patient man. Instead of taking another bus home, he walked twenty miles back home to save on bus money. His intermittent employment required him to report early in the morning at the pier, where he would then be transported from a small boat to a large international shipping vessel. His salary of twenty-five U.S. cents a day, whenever he got the chance to work, quickly vanished. We paid ten pesos, which is equivalent to one dollar a month, for the space beneath the house.

To make our house livable, my father made us a front door. He nailed wooden strips from discarded fruit crates onto a frame of a thin panel, using—two-inch-wide and four-inch-long pieces of old wood. When he was done cutting, hammering, and nailing the flimsy pieces of wood to fit the opening of our crawl space, my mother took over. She meticulously polished and buffed the front door to a lustrous sheen by making paste wax from melted candle drippings mixed with kerosene. She used this to shine everything that my father had made out of plywood and bamboo. Adults had to stoop low to enter the crawl space through the front door. The crate swung inward with a sharp, cracking sound toward the living area, making the small entryway into a tiny, usable space. In a high-pitched voice, my mother continually reminded my brothers and sisters and me, "Ning, Tino, Linda, Lina, Tessie, Boy, and Shirley, please keep the door closed. Keep the flies out!" Besides the flies, there were tarantulas that lived in the rafters, and scorpions that nested in the dirt beneath our feet

A mock-up of the crawl space Ning grew up in

Our Living Space

The size of our living space was 10 feet by 12 feet—barely enough to accommodate nine of us: five girls, two boys, and my parents. We all learned to maneuver around each other in the cramped space like a flock of pigeons flying through the city in a synchronous dance, sensing the exact location of one another as we moved around without colliding. Adults were unable to stand up with full body extension in the house. Only the children could move easily through the room, playing with toys that our father had made from recycled tin cans. I remember the tin stove, dishes, and cups he made for me. I played with and cherished them for a long, long time.

Mother hand-stitched a curtain made from thin, brightly colored scraps from old cloth and hung it from an overhead beam. This curtain separated the dark open space into rooms, to give the illusion of privacy and playful optimism.

As you entered the front door and took one step into the crawl space to the right, a sheet of recycled quarter-inch plywood provided seating for our family and visitors. In the daytime, this was used as a work table and a play area. At night, the same plywood platform served as a bed for five of us: my mother and father, my sisters Lina and Tessie and my youngest baby sister, Shirley. Directly next to the plywood bed, to the right, was another sleeping area, which was cobbled together with bamboo strips attached to a framework, made from salvaged pieces of wood. I slept there with my oldest sister, *Ate'* Linda (*Ate* is a prefix used before a name to address an older sister) and, my two younger brothers, Boy, and Tino.

Both of the beds were elevated one foot off the ground by a low platform and we used the area below to store our best leather church shoes, and sandals my father had made from rubber tires. Between the beds, another panel of brightly patterned scraps of fabric hung as a privacy curtain, which was completely ineffective as a partition, but the good intentions were enough to preserve a little modesty.

> **A home is a place dirty enough to enjoy and clean enough to be healthy.**

On one wall, clothing and diapers were folded in tidy, even stacks on shelves made of thin pieces of plywood cut into short lengths. The shelves continued to the corner of the room and were covered by patchwork curtains. These curtains were a practical necessity for concealing personal items. They were also a nostalgic diary of memories in colorful fragments of cloth, reminding us of many celebrations. Occasionally, my mother would stand in front of the curtains and point out small squares of cloth, reminiscing about various friends that had given us their clothing and the Christmas parties and birthdays for which they were worn.

Our living space was so small that when my father sat on the plywood bed, the distance from the top of his thick, black hair to the ceiling was about twelve inches. When he sat on the corner of the bed, his knees grazed the bench, by the kitchen table, made from salvaged two by four scraps of lumber.

Near the kitchen table, my father had installed a metal light fixture suspended by a hook between the under beams of the house. He hung the light as a symbolic gesture of prosperity, hoping the presence of the empty light fixture would transform our dark, cramped space into a comfortable home, like our cousins' upstairs. Our family was too poor to afford a fluorescent light bulb or electricity and my father's frequent scavenging missions to the pier hadn't produced an intact fluorescent tube that fit the fixture. The light remained empty for several years, collecting layers of dirt and grime. He secretly hoped that a visiting relative or a generous friend would notice the absence of a light bulb and give us one as a gift someday. His wish eventually came true in exchange for his other talent as a natural healer.

One evening at dusk, a construction worker came by our house with a severely dislocated arm. The injured man was referred to my father. My father was well-known and a respected healer in the community. He has a remarkable ability to help heal broken bones.

The injured man introduced himself as Mang Jose, and thanked my father for his help. He had fallen from a ladder at his construction site, and needed immediate attention. He was invited into our candlelight crawl space, where my father carefully manipulated the man's hanging and broken shoulder back in place and applied some boiled guava leaves around the affected area. A sling was made from an old cotton sheet to cradle Mang Jose's broken shoulder and it was then tied securely around his neck. He thanked my father for his help, and went home very happy.

My father never charged anything for his services. He believed that his gift of healing would not be as effective if he took any monetary compensation for it. He believed that God would provide.

The Gift of Light

The next day Mang Jose, the same man, came back with a gift. He brought a new fluorescent light bulb to illuminate our crawl space so he can; too, benefit from it should another accident happen to him again. Father was overjoyed and thanked him repeatedly. He held the long, white glass tube very carefully by the metal ends to keep it from shattering, and carefully laid it on a clean cloth on the plywood bed. He told us to stay in safe distance away while he ran upstairs to my Aunt and Uncle, *Tia' Bennie* and *Tio' Indong's*, house.

We all stood frozen in place, staring at the highly valued light bulb with a mixture of excitement and fear. From upstairs, he quickly threaded a borrowed thin extension cord through the floorboards down to the crawl space below, and then ran downstairs to delicately slip the light bulb into the fixture. In a moment of silence, he proudly pulled the metal chain, and the bluish light flickered on with a soft buzzing sound. We all grinned with delight and applauded the miracle of light that shined brighter than my grandmother's hand-made candles that we were normally accustomed to. For weeks, our friends and relatives would stop by at night bending down into the crawl space to admire our newly lighted home. Father's prayer had been answered.

> **Ask in silence. In due time, you will be answered.**

Beneath the fluorescent light in our crawl space, on a thin shelf was our most prized electronic possession—an old, old radio from World War II. It was an electronic relic of metal and plastic that comes to life as the musical heart of our home. My aunt and uncle were kind enough to supply us with electricity by way of an extension cord through our living area, so we could have the modern amenities of music and news.

From the radio, serious voices came out through a crackling noise of static that connected our family to the current events and the music of the '50's and the '60's. Between newscasts and dramatic soap operas in *Tagalog*, (our national language), we enjoyed listening and dancing to American pop music. Mother would turn up the volume on the radio early in the morning to motivate us to start the day with joy. She openly sang to the tune, "Wake up Little Susie," by The Everly Brothers, and "Arimunding-munding," one of her favorite Filipino folk songs. With her back bent low, she swayed from side to side in rhythm with the music. If she could have stood up straight in the crawl space, she would have danced. Over the buzz of the traffic, her duo with the radio was heard by all of us, including my cousins upstairs. This was our morning wake-up call.

> Music uplifts the spirit. It eases away the pain in life.

Our Altar

In our home, to the right of the kitchen table, was the statue of the Mother Virgin Mary. The shrine was over a foot tall, considered large in comparison to our tiny living space. However, it was in perfect proportion to the importance of the Holy Mary's presence in our lives. She was a powerful symbol of our Catholic faith. She represented strength and grace in the midst of our overwhelming hardships. The statue was in a box made from thin salvaged strips of wood curved at the top, like a church window. My father had painted the background behind her with a brilliant blue and the edges that bordered the box, with white. A necklace of *sampaguita*, (our national flower) that smells like gardenia, was draped around the neck of the sacred Virgin Mary.

Mother Mary at the family altar

The Madonna stood in beauty and strength, a white lace embroidered doily under her feet, with wooden rosary beads with a silver cross at the very end encircling her folded hands. She was luminescent in our dark, humble surroundings. We knelt and fervently prayed each day at dusk at her feet, asking that we be blessed with her gift of wisdom and guide us in our daily lives.

Pray about everything, and fear nothing.

Our crowded living space included the Madonna's shrine, the two plywood beds, the kitchen table, and a bed and sheets storage. Next to our main living area was another room. This room was also beneath my cousins' house, which was more exposed to the outside automobile fumes and the constant honking of traffic. This place was where we bathed, washed dishes and kept the pigs, chickens and ducks. A few steps from the pig pens, was where we prepared our meals and cooked on a stove made from an empty five-pound coffee can.

Coffee can use as a stove for cooking

One open end was filled with saw dust pounded and molded to form a circle in the center and one side of the coffee can so the heat from the fire can go through and heat to cook our food. Also directly next to the pigs, was where we bathed by dipping an empty 16 ounce sardine can, called *tabo* into a bucket of water and pouring it over our heads. Out of modesty and a feeling of privacy, all of us learned to bathe fully clothed since there were no partitions between the rooms and the outside alley. After each bath, we poured any leftover water from the bucket over the backs of the pigs. I liked to hear them squeal with excitement as they also shared a bath. Ventilation was critically important in our crawl space. The intense heat and humidity affected the foul-smelling animal pens and the toilet, which was close to our living space. The toilet bowl was made of an empty wooden box that once contained canned food and had been discarded by the market. The toilet seat was a square piece of plywood with a hole cut out of the center and secured on top as the box. The toilet was two feet by two feet square, and one foot deep, lined with a half inch of newspaper that was changed every day. The commode was surrounded on three sides by a flimsy and unstable privacy wall made from pieces of old, bent cardboard. This wall leaned delicately against another cardboard wall that would collapse if brushed by the wing of a wandering chicken wondering by. During a typhoon, the cardboards were destroyed by floodwater and replaced with semi-sturdy tin walls over again. My Father would tear apart empty, recycled metal vegetable oil can with tin snips and would flattened them further into sheets-using a hammer. This would then replace the already bent cardboard until the next typhoon comes. When the tin walls were made, he carefully tipped them up around our bathroom area for a new privacy wall.

Multipurpose and Multifunction Areas

Out of necessity, all areas and surfaces in our house were multi-purpose besides being multi-function. They were very close distance to each other to save valuable space. The plywood bed was used both for seating and sewing surface in the daytime. We ate our meals on the kitchen table, which also become a food preparation and a schoolwork corner. To give you an idea of our living area in the crawl space; from the kitchen table, three steps took us to the bathing area, which was also used for washing dishes, which was also next to the pigpen. One step separated the pigpen from the dish drain board which was also used to store cups, dishes, and other kitchen utensils

We moved through our home in tiny few steps: one body turn from the bamboo slat bed was small, a foot by foot, study bench; two steps from the study bench to the kitchen table;

five steps from the Virgin Mary to the pig pen; one step from the dish drain board to the toilet; three steps from the toilet to the cooking area; two steps from the stove to mother's flower and vegetable garden which was an eight inch mound running the full width of the house. We all learned to adapt and adjust to the small area of our home.

Next to the plywood kitchen table, a flap of green military canvas hung from a beam that created a flexible wall. This wall divided our living space from the outside alley. This flap next to the table created a tiny alcove where *Ate'* Linda, who is my eldest sister, and I were asked to sleep when relatives and friends come to visit. They stayed for at least a week. My parents always welcomed our friends and relatives. They were considered our honored guests when they arrived for some birthday celebrations—christenings and Christmas holidays. Mother had always told us," We should always make room for family and friends. They are God's messengers and they are gifts to us from heaven." From this point of view, the Philippines is known to be the most hospitable country in the world. This is how God gives his tests sometime—opening our door to the needy was a measure, my parents said, of our hospitality.

Sleeping Arrangements

We, the children, were re-shuffled like puzzle pieces, to make room for our relatives from the Nueva Ecija, (province North of Manila). While *Ate'* Linda, my eldest sister and I, slept on the cot next to the musty smelling canvas wall by the kitchen table, my younger brothers, Boy, Tino slept on the dirt floor under the kitchen table. I was scared to sleep, in the dark area, beneath the table where the scorpions nested in the ground dirt. In the rafters above the plywood tabletop was the dwelling place of tarantulas and poisonous centipedes. Sleeping in such close distance to their territory was frightening. We cannot complain because this would mean being selfish and disrespectful to our parents and our guests. I would then lie awake all night, every muscle in my body tense, and I listened in nervous anticipation of the whispering slide of the tarantula's tentacles on either the wooden beams above my head, or on the dirt floor below. I was fully prepared to leap and run if they came too close.

The dark alcove behind the kitchen table was where I learned about the danger of poisonous insects, and arachnids. I was around six years old at that time. The venom injected from a scorpion's tail barb was significantly more painful than a bite from a tarantula or a poisonous centipede. Once, I fell asleep and was jolted awake by a sharp jab from a scorpion sting. The intense pain inflicted by the venom from the scorpion's tail and pinchers swelled my lower leg into a reddened knot that I quietly endured until the following morning. Regardless of the seriousness of the situation, we were taught not to disturb our sleeping family and house guests.

> **Endure the pain and be patient. Your rewards will come sooner than you think.**

Mother cared for my wound first thing in the morning. She began by cleaning and rubbing the swollen area with a swab of cotton sterilized in a boiling pot of water from the tin stove. Then, the viscous gel from an Aloe Vera plant was squeezed onto a cotton ball and dabbed delicately onto the bite. She would bow her head and say a short prayer, "sealing" my injuries with a kiss, and confidently told me that I am going to be all right. For absolute assurance she would repeat, "Everything is going to be just fine now, Ning, Your angel is around helping." My mother gave me a kiss and a hug and she then proceed to the kitchen and started cooking breakfast for the family.

> **A mother's tender and loving care overcomes any pain.**

However, sometimes the confident kiss can be overpowered by a serious infection. For weeks after the scorpion bite, my lower leg became increasingly infected, swollen and throbbing with pain. Mother continued to clean the reddened knot with sterilized water and alcohol, and then gently squeezed the infection from the pustule. She rubbed the powder from a crushed tablet of sulfanilamide, an anti-biotic, into the raw wound. The sting of the medication in my open wound was very painful, and the bite would throb off and on. I healed from the bite, but I was left with a large scar in my right ankle, which left a scar even to this date. My mother's concern for my health and her tender care was one of the fondest memories of this unforgettable experience.

Upstairs in the home of my Aunt and Uncle, *Tia' Bennie* and *Tio' Indong*, the wooden boards of their flooring were loosely spaced. The gap between the boards allowed dirt and coffee spills to filter down onto our heads below. Knowing my father, he made a protective ceiling for us by nailing and pasting recycled newspapers to the beams of our ceiling. This provided a barrier that saved us from the discomfort and yet another cleaning situation.

Occasionally, a moving bulge in our "ceiling" was a sign of the presence of a rodent, prompting a quick action to strike this black ugly rat with a broom. The force ripped the paper and liberated the rat. A chase began, with my parents shoving a broom toward the frightened rat while it ran along the dirt floor frantically looking for an exit. Peace and quiet eventually returned and the shredded section of the newspaper was replaced with a clean section, serviceable once more until the next rodent appears and the incident starts over again.

During the Christmas season, the ceiling was completely transformed. Each year, my father would lead all of us children in replacing all of the stained and soiled newspapers from the ceiling with recycled holiday wrapping paper. For us, this time of the year was an occasion of honor and celebration. My sister and I helped him replace and covered our ceiling with mixtures of dazzling recycled bright wrapping paper, colorful images of angels, intricate nativity scenes, and brilliant color of Santa Claus. In excitement, I started dancing with joy and sing Christmas songs happily as loud as I can. In the evenings, all of us children would gaze at the ceiling in amazement as we were brilliantly surrounded by angels flying above our heads. They were beautiful in the soft, flickering candlelight as our eyelids slowly closed and voices softened, one by one, into sleep.

> Billion stars are more visible in the dark.

Chapter 2

FIGHT FOR SURVIVAL

Lesson Two: Hope is present in the most difficult circumstances.

In the midst of every difficulty, lies an opportunity
Albert Einstein

---

*D*uring the long periods of unemployment from his job, my father became proficient at scavenging building materials from the discarded wooden shipping containers at the pier. The greatest difficulty for him was to find enough money for a jeepney ride (a common mode of transportation) to and from the waterfront. He and Tino, my younger brother, would walk twenty miles to the pier carrying their tools. If father's friend, Angel was at the pier, he would give him a free ride home—which was always a blessing.

Scavenging Adventure

A few times, he and his friend, Tony, who owned an old beat-up truck, would go on a wood-and-metal scavenging adventure. Before sunrise, on the day of the trip, my father would wake up and make a strong pot of coffee for himself and his friend. They would gather a few tools and discuss the strategy for the day. For them, the trip was exciting but exhausting. Often, they would scavenge all day long working in extreme heat and humidity and returning home after dark.

One of my father's friends owned a jeepney, which was a World War II U.S. military surplus jeep that had been re-designed to accommodate passengers and cargo. In the Philippines after the war, unemployed men with ample time and no financial resources sometimes refurbished jeepneys out of necessity. The jeepneys were fabricated from salvaged bumpers, and dented hoods and fenders welded into a rusty, mixed-breed of vehicles. When my father, his friend and my younger brother Tino departed for scavenging trip, they would grin and wave good-bye. My father's friend would then step on the gas pedal of his beat-up clunker and leave a cloud of exhaust fumes billowing into our crawl space as they disappeared into the traffic.

They would arrive at the pier and use only their claw hammers to dismantle the immense plywood shipping containers. After the materials were collected and sorted by size and thickness, my father and Tino would stack the pieces of jagged wood and metal scraps into a teetering pyramid onto the roof of the jeepney. The three men surely had a lot of patience. His friend would secure the stack to his jeep by lashing the bundle inside a cocoon of crisscross ropes. The deep potholes in the road would continuously jar the jeep, and shift the top-heavy load abruptly with a thunderous, cracking boom of the metals and woods. They would make frequent stops and take turns readjusting their load of cargo which would start to lean at a precarious angle. The roads' twist and turns would sometimes cause the frayed ropes to break, but the men's perseverance paid off, and they finally made it home—tired, dirty, and hungry. My father and my brother usually get so excited after the scavenging trip that they talk about it all night. The next day, they both got up early and proudly took an inventory of their newly acquired woods and metals. My father knew exactly what each wood was going to be use for—not to mention, the heavy metals.

My father was a quiet man, especially when he is thinking. He showed his love for us by providing; using what resources he had available to repair things and to do what had to be done to make our crawl space as comfortable as possible. He also repaired the animal pens so that chickens would not escape into our living area. He was a master of inventor finding multiple uses for recycled plywood. Virtually all of our furnishings were made from these layered recycled boards. From these, he made our kitchen table and benches, the beds, dresser, shelves, the toilet seat, and his popular home-made boxes.

> **True giving is letting go of the things you cherished the most.** Francisco Samson, my father

My father's skills in making boxes from pieces of old refurbished plywood were well known and respected by our family and friends. With his basic tools—a hand saw, a pocketknife, a hammer, a hand plane, and some brushes and paints—he created and made decorated boxes of all sizes. He enjoyed making them for practical and for decorative uses.

One day, after a neighbor admired a special box that my father was making for my mother; he gave the box to the neighbor instead. My father's generosity impressed us children. He use to tell us that true giving is letting go of the things you cherish the most, and not just giving the things you just want to discard or throw away. This statement made a lasting impression on me.

Sometimes the important virtue of sacrifice was tinged with unfortunate consequences. That day, Mang Tano, our neighbor, left our home with the wooden box. However, my mother was disappointed that her gift had been given away and, in a voice strained by frustration, she snapped, "You gave this box away when we have nothing. What are we going to use now?" My father always quietly responded, "I'll make you another one," and he did. She soon resigned to the fact that the neighbor might have needed the handmade box more than she had needed. Perhaps the box was meant to be a gift for the neighbor's wife.

> **If everybody in town donates a thread, the poor man has a shirt.** African proverb

Mother's Skills

Providing clothes for our growing family was a continual job for my mother. In our neighborhood, many of the hand-me-downs were too threadbare to pass on to others as presentable apparel. My mother would receive an armful of used cotton dresses, shirts, and pants from our rich neighbors with much gratitude and a smile. She would then begin the process of sorting, choosing and cutting away the most serviceable pieces to reassemble. She would carefully lay out each usable piece of clothing on the plywood bed, smoothing it with the palm of her hand, welcoming it into our home. Her fingers would explore a section of the fabric that might suggest a shirt for one of my brothers or a dress for me or one of my sisters. Those sections unusable for clothing would be cut into squares and stitched together to create some curtains.

My mother's skill as a seamstress was so remarkable. She would hand sew every piece of a garment, never using a sewing machine, using only a single needle and thread. Her efficient use of remnants was even more remarkable. She dressed the entire family with colorful scraps from other people's lives. Through her meticulous hand stitching and measuring, she would aim for a perfect fit. A groom's old wedding shirt might become a dress, a worn restaurant tablecloth, cut into a rectangular pouch and stuffed with the unusable scraps of material would perhaps become a pillow. She made an old necktie into a belt.

The idea of new clothes would stir excitement in all of us. We would be curious about what she would make, and whether it would be in our favorite color scheme. The choice was hers. Whatever clothes my mother made would have to last for at least several years. I would hope that the color and pattern of fabric chosen for a dress for me would be beautiful, and it always was.

Our best clothing and best hand-me-down shoes were carefully cleaned and worn for family portraits taken on birthdays or for First Communions. We did not own a camera. My father bartered his healing gift or his homemade

Ning's first communion

plywood boxes for a professional quality photographs. The photographer, Mang Cario, would invite my family into his studio and arrange us in a dignified pose for the official family portrait, trying different standing and sitting positions to get the perfect picture. When we received the picture, we would all gather around and admire how affluent we looked. My father would show it to our relatives and neighbors, and then my mother would whisk the precious photograph away for safe-keeping. She kept it protected in an envelope in a tin box, within a wooden box, on a high-beam shelf far away from floodwaters and rodents.

An early photograph, before my four youngest siblings were born, captured the ideal image that my parents wanted to project of our family to the world. What the photograph did not reveal was my mother's gracious attempts to keep us clean in our tidy clothes before we left the crawl space for the studio. Beneath our formal clothing and the look of perfection achieved in the family portrait, mother had made our undergarments from worn cotton T-shirts given to her by my cousins. Although the underwear was functional, it was difficult to keep on our bodies because the used and recycled elastic bands were too loose to be in place around our waist. We were expected to wear undershirts and chemise at all times, in spite of the sweltering heat and humidity. We were dressed in handmade clothing, clearly influenced by American contemporary fashion. The picture was taken sometime, in 1949. My father looked handsome, attired in a dress shirt and slacks, and my youthful cousin was in the back row. My Aunt Loring sat in a chair in front of him, wearing a short-sleeved V-necked cotton dress, with open-toed sling back shoes, and she clutched a small leather purse. *Ate'* Linda, my eldest sister, on the left and I, on the right side, stood in front of her with oversized bows in our hair, neatly dressed in identical cotton dresses with ruffled collars and ruffled inset pleats in our dresses. We wore ankle socks folded neatly into cuffs, and

Family dressed for pictures

leather shoes. My uncle Eddie stood to the side of my aunt, dressed identically in a short-sleeved shirt, short pants, and dark leather shoes.

Providing for the Necessities

Providing clothes was more easily resolved than finding enough food to feed seven hungry children and two adults. We all lived with the constant gnaw of hunger, but we gave prayers of gratitude to God for what little we have, and we didn't complain because it was disrespectful. Our meals included eggs from our chickens, plus a small amount of rice, tomatoes, onions and cabbage from the garden, and an occasional "milk fish" from the market. The fish was small, shared among nine people, and when everything was eaten except the fish bones. Sometimes I chose to eat the tail fin, if the only other choices were to eat the eyes or the intestines.

> ## Hunger makes hard beans sweet. Italian proverb

Feeding the pigs was one of my responsibilities. I mixed grain with molasses provided by the factory next-door and added discarded vegetables from the market to feed the pigs. I was hungry, and the sticky mixture smelled alluring. There were times when I paused at the borderline between temptation and responsibility, wanting to take a small taste. But I emptied the contents of the bucket into the pigpen, and inhaled the nourishing scent of food left lingering in the air. The pigs were grateful and responded with a rush of snorting and gulping, and then looked at the bucket for more. The chickens rushed toward me, fluttering in the air in anticipation of their favorite meal—a a scattering of cornmeal on the ground. They were all hungry, and wanted more.

A Broken Bond

Our animals were not pets. We ate and sold them to survive. I developed a bond with them which was broken when my father sold a pig or my mother slaughtered a chicken. My parents were considerate regarding my feelings of attachment, and they made sure that I was not around for the sad moment when an animal was sold or killed. They would make careful arrangements for the slaughter or sale to be done during school hours when some of us, children, were in school.

Chickens were raised to be eaten only on special occasions. We regarded birthdays as a celebration of precious life to be honored with a feast and the food my mother had cooked for birthdays was consumed in an instant. The pigs and the ducks were not raised for us to eat, but were sold to supplement my father's meager income from his job at the pier. Regardless of the small amount of food that my mother would raise in the garden or buy at the market, friends often came unexpectedly for dinner. My parents firmly impressed upon all of us that we should welcome them. She said, "Friends are messengers from God. When they visit, we must always invite them to share our food and share everything we have, be it food, clothing or a place to sleep." These words, unknowingly, began to shape my feelings about my family and community.

> **The more we give, the more we will receive.**
> **Francisco Samson (my father)**

The yearly typhoon season in the Philippines would bring sheets of rain and wind that would flood our living space with a foot of polluted, dunk water. This left only three and a half feet between the water and the ceiling which created considerable challenges for sanitation. During these downpours, we learned to live with the scorpions, tarantulas, poisonous centipedes, stinging red ants, and enormous rats that invaded our living space.

The pigs would constantly shriek and squealed as the storm intensified and the water rose and threatened to engulf them. The excrement from the animal pens, and the wooden box that was used as the family toilet would overflow into every section of our home. However, our adversity would become an opportunity for our chickens and ducks to get more nutrition as they relished every insect and worm that swirled past them on the currents in an undulating tide of food.

Adversities open doors to opportunities

Typhoon winds would whip mango and guava trees into hissing windmills that sent fruits, like missiles, slamming into tin roofs and anything else within their trajectories. Animal pens made of chicken wires would rip apart sending the chickens and ducks scattering into the flooded, humid streets of Manila. The sheet of plywood used for our bed, and buffed to a sheen by my parents, became saturated with water. Every one of us would grab whatever we could—the wok, pots and pans and kitchen utensils—before they floated away on the muddy currents. The typhoon waters would swell the study bench that my father had made for me. It would later be dried and re-polished so it could be used again. And so the cycle went. By the grace of God, a few objects were spared from the yearly cycle of devastation. The Virgin Mary stood high enough to survive the flood waters that rose up to only inches below her feet, and I learned to run fast through the floodwater and rescue my schoolbooks, because they were my only treasured possessions.

Mother's Plan

When the storms would subside and we would begin to clean and dry out what was left of our belongings, my mother would clutched her *walis*, (palm frond broom), and sweep.

She swept mud mingled with human and animal excrement out of our home as if purging an old familiar calamity.

"God is good," my mother would say. "There must be a bigger plan." She would sing and sweep. She would pray and sweep, but she would not cry. One year with urgency in her voice, she spoke of a plan she had devised—a plan that was meant to uplift our family from poverty. She had chosen me, the second eldest, and had told me of her plan.

"Maria Luningning Julian Buenaventura Samson, we are counting on you to study as hard as you can in school and get a good education, so you can get us out of this poverty."

My mother could not read because she had only finished first grade. Her family did not have enough money to send her to school. Still she would cleverly read the pictures from the American comic books given to us by the American workers at the pier. She would make her own stories from the cartoon pictures, pretending to read the lines of text by moving her finger back and forth on the page, to creatively share story-time with us. Her illiteracy became a compelling catalyst that inspired me to pursue an education. I had hoped to read to her and to my own children someday.

My father, on the other hand, could read and had finished fifth grade in school. He read articles from the recycled news-papers, pasted on our ceiling and read from magazines he had been given by his American coworkers at the pier where he worked. My mother, brothers, sisters and I would sit close together on the plywood bed and listen to my father's voice while he loudly read Bible stories to us.

My father taught me how to form letters of the alphabet by writing with a pencil on small scraps of recycled paper. The shapes of letters were familiar to me. I had grown up sur-rounded by neat columns of words on sheets of newspaper that were pasted and attached to the ceiling and the beams of the crawl space. Bold headlines in English demanded atten-tion regarding politics and sports. I would lie down on the bamboo bed and trace the letters in the air, forming each word carefully as I saw it above my head: "Storm disaster in Manila" or "Arnold Palmer, the winner of the U.S. Open Golf Tournament." I will always remember these headlines. I learned each letters and word of these big bold headlines until I was able to read and understand them.

Although my father had taught me the basic reading and writing skills, he hadn't grasped the significance of an education for me. He assumed that I would just get married, have children, and serve my future husband, just as generations of women before me had done.

Chapter 3

A BREAKTHROUGH

Lesson Three: Keep your joy in the midst of all your sorrows.

*E*ducation in the Philippines is not free. The primary grades through college, required financial resources for tuition, resources for books, and money for school uniforms, none of which, my family could afford. My older sister, *Ate'* Linda, had been going to primary school through donations from relatives, but any hope for me and the rest of the children had seemed impossible. Nevertheless, the love of learning to read and write had begun to take root deep within me.

A Miracle

Then a miracle happened. Two American men from a Catholic Charity mission came to our home to talk to my parents. Their objective was to provide free financial school assistance to children from poverty-stricken families. They had heard about my eager interest in learning from an anonymous supporter.

We had an idea that the nun who taught us catechism in the alley in front of our house had something to do with it. I had always helped the Catholic sister, round up the children in the neighborhood every Saturday afternoon. After we were all seated on the ground dirt, she would tell us stories and teach us about Jesus for over an hour. I was always fascinated by all the stories she told us about God. She reminded us that God gave his only son, Jesus. He died for us to save us from our sins. She said that someday we would understand. She always told us, children, to be good and to love each other.

It didn't bother her to give each of us a hug with her long, well-pressed, white clothes. She hugged us each Saturday even though we were poor and living in poverty. One day, she gave all of us big, big hugs, then cried and said good-bye. With tears in her eyes, she told us that she was going home, but that she might be back someday. That was the last time I saw her. I missed her.

The Search

In the meantime, the search was on. Our neighborhood in downtown Manila had few street signs. The two men were lost in a maze of warehouses, apartment buildings, businesses and lean-to shanties. In our neighborhood, American men dressed in suits carrying leather briefcases were a novelty. When they arrived, a long line of curious neighbors and children formed behind them following their every stop and turns. Children and adult neighbors were talking excitedly in Tagalog, our national language. One group of neighbors and onlookers speculated that either something very good or very bad must have happened. The excitement of the day was evident in the smiling faces of all the neighbors, who were benefiting more from watching the tall Americans, than our own family was.

The two American men were sweating from the heat but were still neatly groomed and, dressed in dark blue suits, starched white shirts, and neckties. They were both about six feet tall—very tall men in comparison to the average five-feet-tall Filipino man. The American men stooped low; but still both hit their heads on the underside beams as they came through the five foot opening of our wooden-crate front door. We could tell that they were uncomfortable, sitting awkwardly cramped on the plywood bed. They were very humble. My mother offered them pastries cooked on the coffee tin stove, which they politely ate. For a drink, she offered them murky-colored water in recycled glass canning jars. They politely thanked her again, but drank only a small amount. They were so gracious for what little we had to offer.

My mother and I stared at our guests because we regarded the tall, kind men as angels sent from heaven to help us. We were deeply humbled by their presence and the magnitude of their offering. I had hoped that I was deserving of their program, and that I would be accepted.

> Miracle happens when you least expect it.

They snapped open their leather briefcases and took out pads of paper and pens. One of the men glanced around the room, taking note of the surroundings and our living conditions, including the pig pens, the homemade furniture, and the altar where the Virgin Mary stood. The other man asked my mother several questions about my interest in attending school. I was a shy and a quiet seven year old. He then asked me some questions and very carefully listened to each of my responses. I recall being very nervous, and I kept answering with a "yes, sir," or a "no sir." They wrote down some notes, looked at each other and nodded their heads. Then they paused, look around once more, and talked to my mother. I was asked to leave. I left and went to the other end of the bamboo bed, where I could not hear what was said. After a few minutes, they called me back, patted me on my head, and congratulated me for being a recipient of their mission's educational aid for needy families. Both gentlemen gently put their arms around me and patted my back, reassuring me that everything was going to be all right, just like my mother always said. They added that they would pray for my success in school. I told them that I always prayed and obeyed God and my parents. In a shy, and soft voice, I promised them that

I would try my very best to be good in school and to meet their expectations. They smiled, and then unfolded their tall bodies, hitting their heads once again on the underside beams of the house. They crawled out of our home into the searing heat of the day. By this time, my whole family felt the pain they suffered from the big red bumps and bruises forming on their heads. Their inuries would be a reminder to them of how small our house was.

I was so excited to go to school. I had a new identity as a grade school student. My parents told my aunt and uncle about the support that I would be receiving. They told me not to forget that I was no better than anyone else in the family. They reminded me not to be too proud, and not to boast, because it would hurt people's feelings, and because it would be disrespectful to act in such a way.

Early School Education

At the age of seven, I easily absorbed information about several subjects in school. I was surprised to find out that I knew answers to questions that many older children didn't know. My parents reminded me that, although I was in Section One

(the gifted section of students), I wasn't any better than anyone else. I had learned at an early age that each of us is gifted;
each of us excels in some areas in life, and is weak in other
areas. I had started to notice some of God's gifts in my family
members that I did not have. I had noticed that my cousins
could draw animals and make dioramas out of cardboards,
and I could not. My brothers and sisters could draw pictures
of any kind, like my father could, and I could not. On the
other hand, I enjoyed music and, poetry, and I love science
and numbers. I began to notice that I knew more than other
children my age, and my passion to learn about anything and
everything had started to show. My mother always praised us
whenever we did well. Although she never showed any
favoritism among her children, including me, I started to
shine in my own little ways. I thanked God for my gift.

School was a long distant mile from our home. I have to
walk through congested streets packed with people, honking
jeepneys, buses, and freight trucks that shook the ground as
they roared past me. After school, I had to do household
chores before I could open up my books to study. I helped

around the house, washing dishes and watching over my younger brothers and sisters, feeding the pigs and chickens and watering our small garden. I also helped my older sister, and my mother put the younger children, to bed.

When everyone went to bed, and silence prevailed in our growing household, I studied. In one corner of the room, next to the shelves and the bamboo bed, was my study table made by my father. My dresser was my parents' wooden trunk made of *narra* wood or Philippine mahogany, (our national tree), similar to an oak trunk. It was a hard and old wooden trunk that he and my mother had received from his family as their wedding gift. It was handed down to me, and I use it to store all my books and clothes and other personal belongings. It was precious to my parents so I took very good care of it. The trunk was tipped vertically on end, which created a shelf at the top for my books. I knelt on the ground and used a shelf my father had made inside the trunk as my writing table.

Little by little, one walks far. **Peruvian proverb**

Valued as gold and strictly monitored was a single candle, which provided light for my reading and writing assignments. The candle was made by my grandmother, and was attached with melted wax to an empty sardine tin as a candleholder.

Candle used for my long hours of study

I was allowed a limited quantity of lined writing tablet paper and only one pencil. I had to guard and not lose them or waste these materials; my school supplies had to last me a long while, at least until the end of the school year. This encouraged thrift and efficient study habits. I had discovered that writing in small miniature letters could save me a lot of paper and pencils. In addition, while studying and doing my homework, I had learned to "outrun" the candle through speedy study habits since one candle was all we could afford for the entire month. My habit of writing small continues even now.

My parents kept reminding me that very few children were given the schooling and opportunities that I had been given. They encouraged me to study hard, but to also remember that the greatest value of the gift of knowledge is to share it to help others. The gift should be passed on to make a difference in other people's lives. I took that responsibility very seriously, and I studied very hard. At times, the intense concentration in my studies was helpful in taking my mind and my attention away from our difficult living conditions, not to mention, the mosquito bites on my arms and legs.

> **The greatest value of the gift of knowledge is to share it to help others.** Agripina Samson (my mother)

I helped my family members by tutoring my cousins upstairs at Tia' Bennie and Tio' Indong's house. My aunt and uncle had electricity, a black and white television, a shower, and a flushing toilet. Aunt Bennie allowed me to take a shower after my tutoring was done, knowing that our bathing conditions next to the pig pens, offered no privacy.

After helping my cousin, Oben, with his math and science homework, and after my shower at their house upstairs, I was rewarded by being allowed to watch some television. I enjoyed watching *I Love Lucy,* sometimes, *Bonanza* and, the annual event of the *Miss Universe* pageant. Television held my astonished gaze with the same awe as if I were an astronomer looking into the vast cosmos for the first time. After the programs were over, I returned to my family beneath the house having had a view of an amazing world beyond the crawl space, beyond Manila, across the ocean. I had caught a glimpse of the possibilities for a bright future. Perhaps I could reach into Lucy's world of laughter and perfection and bring my entire family with me. After watching television upstairs, I would then light the candle and open my schoolbooks to study.

> **Education is of no value unless shared and used for the good of mankind.**

My teachers, Miss Dorothy Milo, Mrs. Vicensio, and Mr. Toledo, had noticed my passion for math, reading, and science. They supported my efforts in school, and they all set aside a time to coach and help me prepare to compete in several math, reading, and science events. They nurtured my confidence by asking me to help them in their classrooms. I corrected papers and helped students with their assignments and served as a "big sister." I loved the challenges, and I was driven by the small successes. In so doing, I discovered that I liked to teach.

> **If teaching is your calling, do it with passion.**

Christmas in the Philippines

In the Philippines, December 16, marked the beginning of Christmas. During the *Novena*, (nine days before Christmas), everyone's attitude was uplifted. Each night, around seven o'clock, starting the sixteenth of December, my cousin Oben; my younger brother Tino, and I dressed in our best clothes and paraded through the streets of Manila. We sang Christmas carols (*Kumbang chero*) in front of our neighbors' houses. My older sister *Ate'* Linda, made me a beautiful blue dress with sequins sewn onto a tulle netting over the skirt. I sang and danced with enthusiasm while Tino and Oben acted as my lively backup singers.

Two drums and some maracas accompanied our vocals. All the instruments were handmade by my ten-year-old cousin Oben, who was very resourceful at making things from discarded materials. He made the maracas from dried coconut shells filled with tiny rocks or pebbles, with a stick attached at the end for a handle. The drums were made from empty pineapple juice cans that were covered on one end using different materials for differing sound effects. One drum, played by my cousin Oben, was covered with pigskin which was attached to the open ends of the can by a large and thick rubber band. This was played by my cousin, Oben. The other drum, played by Tino, was covered at the ends using a piece of thick plastic from a discarded tablecloth.

> # To celebrate life is to celebrate the birth of Jesus.

Christmas caroling took us deeper into the neighborhood and we were allowed to go fifteen blocks away from our home to serenade families. Homes were intermingled between the shanties, retail businesses, the molasses factory, open-air markets, and apartments. Singing was fun for us children, and it had a silver lining. The neighbors gave us money for singing our carefully rehearsed songs in the Tagalog language, "Ang Pasko ay sumapit. Tayo ay mangagsi-awit…" (Christmas is here. Let's all sing), and for our Christmas songs sung in English. We had never seen real snow, but one of my favorite songs was "Jingle Bells." We sang with every ounce of our energy, "Dashing through the snow on a one-horsed open sleigh…"

We sang at the doorsteps of every house, whether paid or not. On the other hand, we welcomed money and small change. These were essential to us, so we could buy gifts for our family and friends during Christmas. The Cano's family had an elegant house with an iron gate and security guards. His family's house and other well-to-do homes were decorated with Christmas lights because they were affluent enough to afford electricity. These families were usually generous and kind to our lively ensemble.

> **Make someone happy. It will uplift your spirit; you will feel better and be rewarded in the process.**

We returned to the crawl space to count an impressive amount of money which had been kept securely in my blue dress pocket. Mother praised our efforts and was impressed with our cooperative music group, our never ending energy and our Christmas spirits. On a profitable night, our little band of young children had collected forty pesos, which was equivalent to less than a dollar then; but was sufficient enough to buy gifts for our family and friends.

In the meantime, *Ate'* Linda, Tino and I wanted a snow covered Christmas tree—like the ones we had seen in the movie, *White Christmas*. We had watched some Christmas specials on my cousins' television upstairs. We decided to make a snow-covered Christmas tree out of twigs cut from the guava tree that grew in the yard of Mang Cano, the nice wealthy man down the street. They allowed us to enter their gated property to pick us some tree branches. One practical consideration for the Christmas tree was the size. The tree had to be small enough to fit behind our apple crate door, and not so tall that it would hit the fluorescent light.

> **A creative mind can take you outside the realm of the universe.**

My father painted the twigs in white and grouped them together in an oil tin can weighted down with rocks, so our tree wouldn't fall over with all the activities in our cramped living quarters. He threaded an extension cord from upstairs through the floorboards and attached a string of large, colorful Christmas tree lights that a friend had given him. The lights, attached to the thin, white twigs, were beautiful and transparent. No matter how top-heavy the weight was the large glass bulbs shined and sparkled. A year later, my father was given a set of bubbling lights for our twig Christmas tree. The lights' bubbles cheerfully colored in red, yellow, blue, and green, mesmerized the entire family. The tree remained up and the tree lights turned on up until January 6, the final day of our season, which is known as the "Feast of the Three Kings."

The celebration took on a serious undertone when my parents reminded us that the birth of Jesus was the true meaning of Christmas. My mother spoke solemnly about the birth of Christ—the child who represented the purification of our hearts, the renewal of our faith, and a new hope for a peaceful tomorrow. In the Philippines, during the war, our people, both soldiers and civilians, had suffered brutal attacks and the devastating consequences of severe injuries on their bodies and minds. Men without arms or legs, or men blinded in combat, were commonly seen begging for money on the busy streets of Manila during Christmas. My mother and father reminded us that we should be grateful for our home and our health, and for our family, and our blessings of food. We had so much to be thankful for. They said, "It is more blessed to give than to receive. That is the true spirit of Christmas."

Chapter 4

THE TURNING POINT

Lesson Four: We only grow when we are challenged.

$\mathcal{W}$hen I was fifteen, an event occurred that marked the major turning point in my life. My father suffered a serious head injury in a motor scooter accident. He and his friend were driving to work at the pier. His friend was the driver and my father was the passenger. The driver accidentally hit a big pot hole on the road, flipping the scooter and throwing my father into a concrete curb. The impact of his head hitting the concrete curb fractured his skull, and caused the bones in his head to become tender, like a newborn baby's.

We could not afford to hospitalize him, so my father was brought home. But at home, he became, increasingly incoherent, and we then realized the seriousness of his injuries. He sat immobile on the plywood bed, staring blankly into space, his skin gray as cement. We all felt helpless. The family gathered around him and prayed fervently. We were so afraid that he might die that day. The accident had suddenly forged our family into a different shape, under the emotional pressure of another overwhelming challenge.

> **The pain of the little finger is felt by the whole body.** Tagalog proverb

My Aunt, Tia' Bennie, was a nurse, and she quickly determined that hospitalization was critical for his survival. We could not afford to pay for an ambulance, so he was transported in a jeepney to the closest hospital—the Chinese General Hospital—where he remained in critical condition, for two weeks. My mother, brothers and sisters and I, worried and prayed at the shrine of the Virgin Mary. We prayed that my father would come home to us fully recovered, resuming his place as the generous provider who helped our family, neighbors, and friends in their times of need. But even after several weeks, my father, the man who had healed broken bones, and helped others in their time of need, was now forced to rely entirely upon his wife, his children, and the grace of others for his survival. We all loved him, and to see him suffer was unbearable.

Aftermath of the Accident

Through no fault of my father or his friend driving the motor scooter, we had found ourselves immersed in yet another lesson that tipped our emotional balance. We had to rearrange the responsibilities within our household. The accident undermined our limited finances because we were buying medications, and it tested our spiritual faith once more. My mother's reaction to my father's condition was to overcome her fear with an optimistic attitude, as she had done many times before when she was faced with an insurmountable challenge. Her strong will, faith, and idealism transformed the helplessness that all seven of us children felt into *motivation*. She reassured us that we would be able to survive another difficult test. She sang and swept with her "*walis*," the palm frond broom, as she always did at the most difficult times, and she said softly," God has a plan. Something great is going to happen as a result of all this. Let's wait and see."

> **Sing your troubles away. Music is free medicine.**
> **Agripina Samson (my mother)**

But in spite of my mother's outward strength, I had noticed that she would sometimes withdraw from some of her activities in the crawl space to find a quiet corner of the yard where she would pretend to garden. She would sit on the ground with her back turned away from us, holding Shirley, my youngest sister, close to her chest, and then she would sob and cry as quietly as she could.

To make ends meet, we all took on numerous jobs. Mother washed laundry for neighbors, and my eldest sister helped Tia' Belen, Aunt Bennie's sister, sew clothing for other people. My sister also ironed and cooked for friends to help pay our bills. Lina, my younger sister, helped my aunt sew clothing, and she sold bedspreads and curtains that she had crocheted. Tessie cleaned houses, babysat, and took over my job of feeding the animals. Tino helped my parents by running errands for them. Boy, my youngest brother, was always with my father to protect him should he be struck with a seizure. Shirley, the youngest baby, was everyone's responsibility. I sometimes assembled beads made into rosaries and got paid a penny, for each finished one.

My mother and I woke up every day at 5:00 AM to cook food to sell before school. The construction workers who worked on the apartment buildings in our neighborhood purchased the food we had made. We made *bibingka*, a pastry of rice flour, goat cheese, eggs and sugar, mixed to the consistency of a pancake batter, poured into a clay mold, and cooked on top of the coffee tin stove. Because the stove was so small, only one pastry could be made at a time. We also had made a cantaloupe juice drink by scraping the cantaloupes and mixing the shredded pieces with sugar water. These were sold for a penny, which was equivalent to a quarter at that time. These construction men helped the family income substantially by buying meals from us during those difficult years. They also gave me a lot of valuable moral support so I could persist and work hard to succeed in school.

My father, and our entire family at this time, felt vulnerable. During this difficult time, we were fully embraced by the love and emotional support of our friends, relatives and neighbors. They generously gave a peso or two to my mother, although they had their own financial struggles. Those who had so little to give still gave plentifully to us, teaching me throughout this tragedy that the abundance is not material but is rooted deep within.

> **Your struggles in life are short-lived, but your joy is long-lived.**

Tia' Loring and Tio' Peping, my other aunt and uncle, brought food as a gift to us and helped to babysit Shirley as we focused on our various jobs. Mang Angel, my father's best friend who owned a chicken farm outside Manila, brought fresh eggs and chickens for my mother to slaughter. He also generously paid for the medicine to control my father's seizures, which was critical to his recovery. Angel also paid for my father's hospitalization. He was an angel to my father, true to his name.

Two years after the accident when my father still could not work, I began to realize the urgency for me to financially help support my family. In addition to keeping up with my full scholarship, I found a part-time job working in a lawyer's office as a clerk. I would go to work before or after school. I was in the best position among my family members to work and help pay for our daily living expenses.

My father's recovery was very slow, and he often had epileptic seizures. His quiet temperament had changed into an intense moodiness as he realized the grievous extent of his condition. Accepting his fate was a long journey that was being blocked by his anger, fear and frustration. At one time, he even questioned the existence of God. A year after the accident, the whole family was helpless to do anything to help him feel better, but try to emotionally comfort him, and pray for his recovery. We often times wondered about the lessons to be learned from his accident.

> Each challenge has its own corresponding lesson.

After I finished all my course work and requirements in my last year of college, my college advisor and professor, Mrs. Catalina Aguila, recommended that I apply for a job as an assistant chief financial officer at Clark Air Force Base. She knew that I was qualified for the job. As my advisor in business education, she coached me extensively for several weeks; in preparation for my job interview. She had stressed professionalism in my work, and the importance of a professional appearance.

Cooperative Effort

My aunt, Tia' Belen, responded to the situation in a loving way by sewing for me a green cotton dress suitable for the job interview. With my new dress and my one pair of dress shoes buffed to a shiny luster, my outfit was complete for the interview.

My concern for proper clothing was resolved, but I still had no transportation to take me from Manila to my interview in Clark Air Force Base in Pampanga, which was one hundred miles north of Manila. My father began the task of arranging a ride to the air force base, which was two-and-a-half hours away. Fortunately, two days before the interview, Mang Emilio who was a close truck driver friend of my father's, offered to give me a ride to my interview. He said that he was on his way to his weekly freight deliveries at Clark Air Force Base that same day anyway, and that he would be glad to give me a ride.

What a blessing! Another prayer answered. That early morning trip took us from a hot and humid Manila to Pampanga.

> **We can only reach the top of any mountain if we are willing to climb.**

The immense green truck arrived. It was a multi-colored metal patchwork of dents and repairs, which had survived years of service to its resourceful owner. The driver, Mang Emilio, apologized for the torn seat covers that showed metal springs and shredded stuffing, blackened by years of dirt and oil. To me, the condition of his truck was not important. I was grateful for his offer to take me to my job interview, and I was anxious to begin the trip. Abrupt braking and honking to avoid collisions intensified the bumpy two-and-a-half hour ride. When we arrived, I slid down from the freight truck to the smooth pavement and into the clean, orderly world of the American military Base—Clark Air Force Base. Mang Emilio smiled, gave me his blessings, and waved good-bye.

Standing on the sidewalk, alongside of the building, was a long line of 150 confident men and women ready for the interview. Each waited patiently to apply for the one single job. I took my place at the back of the line. The hot sun and humidity bore down on all of us as we waited our turn for the interview. Each applicant seemed to have carried with him or her impressive resume in a leather briefcase. All I had were several letters of recommendation from my professors and Mrs. Aguila, my advisor.

When I realized that the back of my dress had been blackened by the dirt and sweat resulting from the long ride in the freight truck, I felt a sting of humiliation more intense than the sting that any scorpion had ever inflicted on me. My mind flooded with a sense of futility and an overwhelming doubt about my chance of getting the job, as I stood in the searing sun with the long line of applicants. The responsibility toward my family and to all those who had supported my academic journey created doubt and anxiety too great to bear. I began to pray. asking God to give me a chance at this job so I could support my disabled father, and my struggling family. I promised that I would contribute to all those who had helped me along the way. I would open doors of opportunity for others, as they had opened doors for me. I prayed that I be granted the miracle of getting that job.

> **Often times, we know who we are, but not what we may become.**

The Final Interview

Dr. Escavelle, the chief financial officer, had sorted out all the applications. I had been scheduled for the final round of five applicants. The pressure I had felt was so intense that I wanted to retreat to a private place away from all the people in the office. There was no place to go where I could be alone, so I wedged my body into the clean white corner of the reception room and brought my hands up to my face to pray. I prayed and cried, with the back of my dress still wet from a frantic attempt at cleaning the stain.

Finally, he made a decision. He thanked the four other men and women, and called me into his office. I was the last one interviewed. There, he looked directly into my eyes from across his desk and smiled. He offered me a seat. I took it. I slowly lowered my whole body to the seat, hoping that he would not notice the stain on the back of my clothes. With empathy in his voice, he said that he recognized some similarities between us. My situation was similar to his own life growing up in the Philippines. He came from similar circumstances and had noticed my hungry and sincere effort which needed to excel in an environment filled with challenges and obstacles. He told me that his choice was based on character qualifications for the position as well as academic achievements. He then added that my professors' recommendations showed that I was on my way to receive the highest honor in college in just two weeks. He told me that I had earned the position with perseverance and with a tenacious spirit. At the end of the interview, he did noticed and comment on the condition of my clothing, saying that the dress revealed a multitude of life journeys.

I thought that I was dreaming. Another miracle had happened. Dr. Escavelle hired me as his assistant. He was a gentle, benevolent mentor. He changed the course of my life that very moment, by placing his trust in my abilities. He gave me the rare chance to flourish. The impossible dream had become real.

I remained good friends with him, his wife and his children, for many years, until his death.

> ## To be humble is to show your real self to God.

My parents had cautiously received the news of my new job, whispering to me that my employment was a prayer answered. However, the news had to be kept a secret. My father was afraid to talk to his friends and family about my job. He was concerned that talking about it would mean that he was being boastful, and that could cause me to lose the job before I even started. My mother, however, was excited and proud when I received my first paycheck. She couldn't wait to tell the construction workers, who daily bought our food. Wihout their overwhelming support, we would not have had food on the table for ourselves, medicine for my father, and school supplies for us, children. My mother helped me prepare a huge basket filled with the construction workers' favorite food and juice drinks as a thank-you gift. Tino, my younger brother, helped us deliver the food to their work site. They all gathered around us with smiles on their faces, shaking hands and hugging us. I was so happy to be able to give back with what little gifts I had for them, compared to what they have given us during those hard times. They surely made my day.

> **Don't forget to look back to where you came from or you will never reach your final destination.**
> Agripina Samson (my mother)

"Ning, you didn't forget us. You came back to say hello— even with your new important job. We knew you would make it because you worked and studied so hard to achieve it," one construction worker said. I thanked them for their encouragement and the unconditional support they had given to my family. Their kindness had sustained me since the young age of seven. The food and the juice drinks they had purchased for many years had been critically important for our survival. Because of my father's disability, during those lean years, we barely had enough food to make it for a day. With their patronage, we were able to make it day by day. To reciprocate their kindness, I kept in touch with them and their families and gave them some assistance whenever I had a chance to come to my homeland.

News of my job traveled quickly throughout our neighborhood. Despite my father's concerns about the news of my job being boastful in the eyes of others, most of our neighbors and friends were very pleased and proud of what I had accomplished. I would come home to Manila for the following three years with gifts of appreciation to let everyone know their significance in my life. I tried to show my deepest respect for them, and for my humble roots.

Chapter 5

THE HARVEST

Lesson Five: It is possible to live your dream. Dream the impossible.

In Celebration

*W*e had planned a party. My mother had decided to combine two important celebrations, my eighteenth birthday and my new job.

Tia' Bennie, my aunt, told my mother about debutante' parties which she had read about in the society section of the newspapers. She described photographs of parties given on the eighteenth birthday of young women as an acknowledgment of a significant milestone in their lives. Mother liked that idea and decided that, with my new job, I could afford a little debutante' party.

All our birthday parties had always been given in our crawl space; however, this celebration would be different. My mother decided that this important event should be held in a restaurant, to comfortably accommodate at least twenty guests. This way, our family, friends, and other guests, would have ample room to move around. Relatives and friends arrived at the restaurant dressed for a feast, dressed in their best church clothing. They told stories and sang Filipino songs. Tia' Belen sewed me a special sleeveless dark teal dress sewn of fine brocade fabric. She gave this to me as her gift.

The guests reminisced and told the same stories that had been repeated over the years about my growing up. My father had told of my near-fatal drowning accident at five, which occurred while I was on his back during one of our outings to the Pacific Ocean. My mother talked about my various jobs and certificates I'd received or won for representing my school in different conferences and competitions. The party was an occasion when good storytelling was entirely appropriate. The guests asked teasing questions about my boyfriends, but everyone knew my life was narrowly focused on my studies and my work.

Ning receiving an award for competition

My father had arranged for a photographer to attend the party. He snapped a shot at the very moment I leaned forward to blow out the eighteen candles on my cake.

Ning's eighteenth birthday

I was surrounded by my friends and relatives and class-mates. My father, although easily fatigued from the accident of the previous year, had maintained his important presence as the head of the family, and he led a toast for "long life and success." Everyone raised their glasses of juice and soft drinks towards me, and yelled, "*Mabuhay* (long live) and Happy Birthday to Ning Ning!"

That day was a memorable day for everybody. We were all happy that we could all be together for that special celebration. I felt so blessed on that important day of my life. It had been the very first party that my family had celebrated outside our crawl space. It was great!

From the Crawl Space to Clark Air Force Base

The day had arrived for me to pack my belongings and move from the crawl space to the air force base to start my new job. I carefully wrapped two small plaster statues, one of the Madonna and one of Jesus. I carefully handled and wrapped them in white cotton cloth and packed them safely between my new work dresses made by my aunt. I then latched my suitcase with joy and I thought about the lessons that my parents had taught me.

> **We can do no great things, only small things with great love. Mother Teresa**

My mother had a profound effect in forming the values that anchored me as I faced the challenges of growing up under difficult circumstances. She spoke simply and directly to me with love, encouragement, and optimism. Her confidence in my abilities had sustained me through many years of rigorous studies.

Early Lessons in Life

The earliest lessons that my mother taught me were those of encouragement. She helped me to cope with difficult challenges by maintaining a positive point of view. I was born with a congenital hand defect. I was often teased by other children while growing up. The fingers on both my hands were clasped into a tight fist, like a crab. My mother helped my hands to function normally by slowly massaging and prying my fingers open each day. After my hands were pried open, my mother or my father would place a small piece of cardboard on my palm, as a mold and support. The cardboard was securely bound together with strips of cloth, with my hand flattened between the cardboard. This was very painful, but eventually the muscles elongated, and I was able to use both hands like everyone else in my family.

When children teased me, my mother would give me comfort with a simple story of encouragement told from her heart: "Ning, they teased you when we had to bind your hands in cardboard, and later they teased you about your double-jointed hands and called you "crab claws." Someday you will accomplish great things with your hands, Ning. The children tease you because you are tiny. You are always the shortest in your class and you will be for a long time. Just ignore them. Even though you are the tiniest, you will be the best, always, in all your classes—if you believe. Remember that! Look at ants. They are very tiny but carry great weight on their backs. They work together. They can move fast in mounds. You are like that. If you work hard then you can be whatever you want to be. Think of all the things small people can do. Small people can get into tiny spaces that big people can't, and they don't hit their heads so often either!"

> **To prosper is to plan, to take action, and to stay positive.**

Father's Gift

My father's gift to me was his constant demonstration of values held quietly in his heart. He spoke few words, but he always demonstrated his compassion and willingness to help friends and strangers, regardless of the scope of their needs. He helped form my core values when he reminded me that all people are equal. He repeatedly reminded all of us children that each one of us could contribute our own unique, personal gifts to enrich the lives of others. He spoke through his hands when he created a small, beautiful brown box made from scraps of wood. When he gave it to me, the gesture proved that God's love was alive in the offering.

> **A gift that counts is the gift that comes from the heart.** Francisco Samson, (my father)

Ning's Father

I had to leave my family, and I tried to contain my tears. My father had taught us to conceal our emotions to show strength in front of the younger children. This was emotional stamina that my father had practiced through his lifetime of loss and disappointments. My parents remained calm in the crawl space until I dipped through the front door and stood up outside, holding my suitcase, and then we all clung to each other and cried.

My father had made arrangements for my transportation to Clark Air Force Base, to take me into a lifestyle with customs completely foreign to me. I was scared. On the other hand, I was ready for a change.

During the long two-and-a-half hour drive, I had time to reflect on my life. Against all odds, and with God's grace, my life events had oftentimes opened the door to the next opportunity. It had been a remarkable moment when the American men from our church had found my family living beneath my aunt and uncle's house and gave me a chance to flourish in school. I was extremely fortunate to have had the level of encouragement and support from my teachers and professors who gave their time and effort to help me in school. I was grateful to the invisible forces of prayer and miracles that must have intertwined at a precise moment, to place me in the office of Dr. Escavel, whom I considered my angel. He changed my life forever. My success was theirs.

> **The only way to discover the limits of the possible is to go beyond them—into the impossible.**
> Arthur C. Clark

I arrived at Clark Air Force Base where I was warmly welcomed by Mang Santos, my Filipino sponsor and his family. I lived with them for three months until accommodations opened up in the civilian housing area. My host family served as a safe cultural bridge between the Filipinos and the Americans. They generously helped me adjust into the unfamiliar lifestyle on the base.

Suddenly, my surroundings had dramatically changed. I was used to the crushed masses of people, pungent animal smells, and the noisy traffic and polluted exhaust fumes in downtown Manila, where my life was squeezed into a small, dark space. In contrast, on the base in Pampanga, I was lost in all the bright, open space. I felt like a mouse reacting to sunlight by wanting to run into a dark corner for protection

The American military base was an extraordinarily different world built on a clean orderly structure of massive buildings. It was considered the biggest U. S. Military air base overseas before it closed in the nineties. The roads were wide and smoothly paved. There were two Olympic-sized swimming pools, movie theaters, a shopping center, hobby shops, the BX: (Base Exchange), and a well-manicured and a spacious golf course.

When I first saw the golf course, it took me back to reading the newspaper headlines above our heads on the ceiling of our old house under the crawl space: golf tournaments, Jack Nicklaus, Arnold Palmer. The game of golf had no significant value or meaning to us, living in a tiny crawl space. My host family explained that golf was a popular sport played on that course by rich American generals, military officers, and well paid civilians working on base. So it was.

I was homesick. Every weekend, I would take a bus home to spend time with my family. My mother and I would talk constantly. We talked and washed clothes, hung the clothes on the clothesline to dry, and talked some more. She would tell me elaborate stories about each one of my brothers and sisters and how they were doing in school and how much she appreciated my help with their tuition, their rent, and all their household expenses. Then she asked about my life on base and my job.

> **Live for the moment. Don't dwell on yesterday's sorrows; instead, thank God for all his blessings.**
> **Agripina Samson**

The lifestyle differences between the Filipinos and the Americans on the base were inconceivable to my mother. I told her that I would invite her to an American movie theater on base, where she could sit in a comfortable velvet chair and watch a film, munch on a big bag of popcorn smothered with butter, nibble on a giant candy bar, and drink a super-sized cup of soda while watching the movie. I told her that the roads on base were wide and smoothly paved, with no potholes, and the streets were not congested, compared to downtown Manila. She was most amazed when I told her about the abundance of food on base. She listened to me carefully, clicking her tongue and shaking her head in dismay when I told her that Americans would throw leftover food away in garbage cans when they were finished eating. Mom said, "They could have saved it and given their leftovers to their pets—better yet, to their chickens and pigs." I told her that, they don't do that on base. I remember her telling us, "Finish your food. Children are starving all over the world. We are lucky that we have food on the table."

After a month of living with Mang Santos's family, I was notified that a place in the civilian housing area had become available. I packed my suitcase and moved into an enormous metal Quonset hut occupied entirely by Filipino civilian employees. The Quonset hut was a vast open space with an arched semicircular ceiling made of corrugated metal. Bunk beds lined each side of the room. Each bed's coverings were smoothed down and perfectly tucked in at the corners, and the beds were arranged into long orderly rows. The majority of the women spoke Tagalog, reminding me of my neighbors and relatives at home.

The women living in the civilian housing area were employed as cooks in different housekeeping trades, or in clerical or technical jobs. I had to keep my position a secret and practiced what my father told me about humility. The women workers all worked to support their families, but I was afraid problems might arise if my administrative position was mentioned. I told them, when asked, that my job involved working at the Processing Center as an accounting technician. After work, I quietly slipped into my bunk bed and went directly to sleep to avoid more questions.

It was at this job that allowed me to receive my very first official paycheck. I was jumping with joy, holding my check up in the air and saying to myself, "Thank you, Lord. Now I can financially help my family." I suggested to my parents that the family should move to an apartment with electricity, bedrooms, a kitchen, and a bathroom. In addition, I was glad to be able to continue paying for the tuition of my brothers and sisters so they could attend school. I hoped that my support would also open up new possibilities for my brothers and sisters' futures.

Everyone except my father was excited about moving into an apartment with tall, solid walls and concrete floors, which would be easier to clean than the dirt floors of our crawl space. My father stubbornly resisted the idea of change, and he refused to move. He said that he was content where we lived.

In a moment of bruised pride, he said, "and besides, the man is supposed to support his family."

> **I dreamed a thousand new paths; I awoke and walked my old one.** Chinese proverb

"What's wrong with you? My mother said with disappointment. "Now that Ning has a job and she can help us, you don't want to move? You stay here with the pigs and scorpions. The rest of us will go!"

A suitable apartment was located three blocks away, on Misericordia Street, in Manila. My father resisted the move because he had humbly survived hardships alongside those around us and was afraid of being viewed as "superior" by relatives and friends. However, his best friend, Mang Angel suggested that living in a bigger home and having more money would allow my father to be more generous. The idea of giving more to others appealed to him, so he begrudgingly sold the pigs, and agreed to move three blocks away.

The apartment was located at a street level in a concrete building. My parents moved their few belongings and my mother immediately planted bright pink cosmos in the raised concrete planters by the entry way. She could finally afford to buy vegetables at the market; so she no longer had to rely on using every inch of soil in the planters for the cultivation of food.

The apartment was on two levels, separated by ten steps. The upper portion had two bedrooms, and the lower level was an open space, which included the kitchen, dining room, and living room. Everyone enjoyed a new sense of freedom. The younger children twirled in circles with their arms outstretched, showing their appreciation in smiles.

My parents bought new furniture for the first time in their lives. They proudly gestured toward their new dining room table and chairs, a sofa, lamps, and a clock that looked like a sunburst, made of gold-painted metal. They had experienced their first real beds, a gas stove and a refrigerator, and new cups and china dishware. My father was pleased by the convenience of electricity in the apartment. The light made it easier for him to see, when he made wooden boxes and the living room had a television set, which I bought secondhand from a departing military family.

The kitchen was an answered prayer for my mother. She had more pots and pans than ever before in her life. She had a gas stove with four burners to cook with, which was especially helpful when we had our large family gatherings. The cupboards began to fill with new drinking glasses which replaced the tin cans and chipped, recycled empty canning jars we had used before.

My mother displayed her new cream-colored china with a silver leaf pattern in a row on the knickknack shelves that father had made. She used her new china only when guests came to dinner, on birthdays or on special occasions. She would carefully transfer each plate to the dining room table with reverence, the way an altar boy would carry plated wafers to a priest.

I gave my parents an anniversary gift for their dining room—a woodcarving of the "Last Supper" that had been intricately carved from a single, forty pound piece of *"narra"* (our national tree) wood. My parents were overjoyed by its intricate beauty. However, because of my father's concern that the Last Supper wood carving would get dirty, he wrapped it in multiple layers of plastic until it was almost impossible to tell what was beneath. It hung on the wall, collecting dust, mold and oil residues from cooking between the layers of plastic for many years.

Moving to the Hill Hacienda

While I was living in the quonset hut, housing became available in the Hill Hacienda, an area on base that was designated to house civilian teachers, American civilian personnel, military officers, and their families. When I arrived, I was startled to see a spacious, pale green bungalow that looked like a mansion. The peaked roof of the house sloped to a wide veranda or front porch, and was supported by two big square columns. There were two large glass windows on each side of the front door, and they were hung with clean, sheer white curtains.

The house faced an enormous park, where fire trees were planted, with military precision in neat rows. The brilliant orange upturned petals of the blossoms of the fire trees resembled the flames of a fire. For a while, I thought I was dreaming.

> Today's dream can become tomorrow's reality.

I stood on the veranda at the front door with a house key in my hand, having no idea how to use it to unlock the door. I jabbed the key at the lock several times until the front door opened, and then I entered what looked to me like a mansion. I stood in the center of the huge living room, holding my cardboard suitcase and a rolled grass mat under my arm. I felt so insignificant in the enormous space. I looked up at the tall cream-colored walls that intersected solidly at the ceiling, and noticed that there were no dark open spaces for the tarantulas to enter.

> Education can be a solid foundation for fulfilling your dreams.

For the majority of people in the Philippines, the cost of glass windows for homes was prohibitive. I had never been in a home with glass windows, until then. For my family, the only windows were the air spaces between the wooden slats, through which we could see an endless stream of people passing by. The homes and apartment buildings in my former neighborhood were built for tropical conditions, with open rectangular spaces as windows, some covered with translucent panes of *capiz* shells (oyster shells, flattened and cut to fit window squares) or black iron grates.

I stood in my first new American-built home and looked out the clean, glass windows. I began to see new possibilities that would eventually fill every part of my life with light, as if I were seeing into my future through my new glass windows.

The amount of space inside the bungalow seemed wasteful for only one person. I then realized, with some guilt that my entire family and my relatives from Manila and the Nueva Ecija province could all live comfortably in this massive house. The two-bedroom home was completely furnished with elegant furniture, beds with bed linens, a refrigerator, and gas a stove. The kitchen was fully stocked with pots and pans and cooking utensils. In addition, I had access to a Filipino cleaning lady and a gardener.

Chapter 6

CHANGES FOR THE BETTER

Lesson Six: Change is a good sign of progress.

Periods of Adjustment

$\mathcal{A}$dapting to my new environment was overwhelming. I didn't know how to use the knobs on the water faucets, in the kitchen and in the bathroom because they didn't resemble anything I had ever seen. The handles were large plastic knobs with the letters "H" on the right knob and "C" on the left knob. After many attempts at pushing, pulling, and turning the knobs, a stream of water blasted from the nozzle. I felt the running water with my fingers and realized the knobs regulated the water temperature—"H" for hot water and "C" for cold water. Later, the housekeeper explained to me that combining both the hot and cold knobs at the same time would give me warm water. That was a real lesson for me.

At home, the situation of water temperature and faucets was simple. Murky-colored water ran through a metal pipe that protruded two feet from the ground. A metal handle turned the water off or on. There was no hot water in the faucet. Hot water was heated on the coffee tin stove, and the water coming from the metal pipe was lukewarm, not cold.

In my new environment, the main ceiling light brilliantly lit my bathroom. The porcelain sink had a rectangular mirror above it, lit by a bright fluorescent light. I thought of how my father had patiently waited two years before he received a fluorescent tube for the empty light fixture at home. The porcelain shower and bathtub were surrounded by immaculate white tile which was scrubbed to military standards. It was the most beautiful bathroom I had ever seen.

I took my first shower in my new home in complete privacy. I showered for a long time, fully clothed, as I had been taught to do at home. This secluded shower was a luxury item to me in comparison to our exposed bathing area at home, where stream of passers-by could see us taking a shower. While I thought about my past during this lengthy shower, every room in the entire bungalow was filled with a thick white cloud of steam. I was not aware that the second switch in the bathroom was for venting steam.

American beds were huge, soft, and uncomfortable for sleeping, but perfect for jumping on as a trampoline. Although I was the new "assistant financial officer," I was still a teenager. I bounced from corner to corner of the big bed, feeling like a child, filled with excitement about my new home. The transition from a hard sleeping surface to a soft mattress was uncomfortable. I was accustomed to sleeping on a woven grass mat called *banig*, on a firm bed made from bamboo slats. At home, five of us children squeezed together on the bamboo bed, each lying on our sides with knees drawn up to our chests, resembling five prawns on a bamboo tray. From force of habit, I slept in my new giant bed in the prawn position for eight hours each night, without moving.

At home, I had rolled up my grass mat up in the morning and stored it vertically against the closet wall, and had gone about my day. But in my new house on base, no one had told me how to make an American bed the next morning. With no training, I lay very still on my back in the middle of the bed and carefully pulled the sheets up to my neck, neatly folded a cuff, then gently slipped sideways out of the bed. In spite of my careful movements trying not to wrinkle the sheets, the bed still looked messy with waves of white folds. When I first met the Filipino cleaning lady, I stood by her side and carefully watched her as she showed me how to make the bed.

Two of my thin work dresses, my cardboard suitcase, and my straw-sleeping mat-rolled tightly into a tube occupied an otherwise empty clothes closet. My bedroom had a large, mirrored dresser with seven wide and deep, empty drawers. The eighth drawer held a few of my personal items that were, out of habit, neatly folded and wedged into the corner to conserve space. I had wondered then why Americans needed so much room for everything, and why they needed so many drawers for their clothes.

On my bedroom wall hung a few family photographs—pictures that had been protected from several typhoon floods.

The small-framed pictures looked so small and seemed so lost in the broad expanse of wall space. I felt the same way—lost in my new surroundings. The ceiling seemed as far away and as vast as the sky.

The top of the dresser was a perfect location for an altar. I solemnly unwrapped my plaster statues of Mother Mary and Jesus Christ and carefully arranged them on a white crocheted doily in the center of the dresser, grouped with my rosary, a silver cross, a prayer book, and white candle. This altar looked like a miniature version of our shrine at home. My altar was like an anchor of prayer, profound faith, and hope in my new surroundings.

> **We cannot hold a lantern to light another's life without brightening our own.** Chinese Proverb

Mother and Sister's First Visit

It took me just a couple of minutes to put my personal belongings into my dresser and about a second to hang my two office clothes in the closet. After a couple of weeks of getting use to arranging, rearranging, and some more re arranging of the furniture, not to mention, getting lost in my big house, and getting used to the routine, my mother and younger sister, Tessie, came for an overnight visit. As they carefully entered the front door, they both took their sandals off and put them outside the door. As they stood back up, my sister's eyes opened so wide that you could see the whites of her eyes, and my mom's arms reached up to the ceiling and she said, "W*ow*! Ning, this house is like a castle. This is so big and roomy. You can fit the whole family in here with no problem." With her mellow voice, she continued, "This is God's gift to you. I know you will take good care of it. I love it." They both gave me a sighs of unbelief and slowly walked and tiptoed through each room in the house, looking up and down at the walls, amazed by the size and beauty of the house and its furnishings.

"It's so *big*; it's so *big*. It's a *gift* from God!" my sister said.

My mother was curious about the big black opening called the fireplace, and asked if it was used for cooking. I told her, "I don't know, Mom; I guess you can cook on it. It seems like somebody already did. It had residues of burnt wood on it."

Tessie brought me hand-stitched pillowcases as a gift, and Lina, my younger sister, who did not come with them, had crocheted a bright orange-and-white bedspread filled my empty bedroom with a burst of color, similar to the brilliant blooms of the fire tree.

After the tour of the house, my mother took a long, long shower, fully clothed, as usual, and cheerfully sang a duet with her echo in the bathroom. Both Tessie and Mom did not want to use the hot water. They were afraid to get burnt. Besides, they were so used to a cold, lukewarm water temperature. That night, I offered my mother and sister the soft bed in the other bedroom; but they were afraid to sleep alone, so we all slept clustered together in one bed, as we had done for so many years.

After two months of living alone in this mammoth house, I was joined by a roommate. Besides sharing expenses, she eased the loneliness that I had felt without the familiar chatter of people and animal sounds. Susan was an American language arts teacher, whom I had met months earlier at the Base Education Center, where I taught business classes and Tagalog for the United States Air Force Institute. She was pleased that we had been paired up as roommates, and she transformed the empty house with some feminine touches: she replaced the white military curtains with ruffles, and she hung a beautiful oil painting of a brilliant sunset on the living room wall.

Susan patiently taught me how to use the gas stove and the oven, which I had been afraid to use for fear of breaking them or setting the house on fire. For my first lesson, she had taught me how to boil water on the stove. That was easy. Then she taught me how to boil an egg. That was fun. I didn't know it was that easy. I feel like my mom. As time went by, I became more and more familiar with using the stove and the oven, and I started the adventure of trying my own Filipino recipes such as the *leche' plan* (custard pie), a*dobo* (a chicken dish marinated in soy sauce, vinegar, garlic and peppercorns slow cooked to a nice consistency), and *pancit*, (rice noodles). I began to be more of a homebody, cooking and eating at home, instead of eating out. Susan and I became the best of friends, and I was not quite as lonely anymore.

My accounting job was a gift, laden with responsibilities, which I accepted with gratitude. I poured myself into the job working as many hours as necessary to complete my duties for the air force which also provided an opportunity for three additional jobs. I taught Tagalog, our national language, and typing, to military men and women in the evenings. I also collected dues for all the military clubs on base including the Officers' Club, the NCO (Non-commissioned Officers' Club), and the Airmen's Club. In addition, I started auditing the books for an additional job. I didn't get home until 11:00 o'clock at night. By the time I got home, it was time to get ready for bed.

I have enjoyed all my full-time and part-time jobs. They have kept me busy, and I have earned a substantial amount of money, which has enabled me to financially assist my family in Manila. My mother and father were counting on me and I didn't want to disappoint them. I had become the sole breadwinner of the family. My eldest sister, *Ate* Linda earned only a part-time wage as a canteen helper in the Department of Justice. My younger brother, Tino, just accepted odd jobs at the pier, while going to school at night. The rest of the children were all finishing their elementary and high school educations. Just like I mentioned before, in the Philippines, we have to pay for our education. We don't have the advantage of the American educational system, where a free education is available to every child. We are so blessed here in the United States.

Language Similarities

My evening classes were well attended by American military and civilian personnel who wanted to learn basic conversational Tagalog. I focused on the conversational part of the lessons, so the students would learn how to carry on a conversation during their stay in the Philippines. I covered the proper pronunciation of the language, which sounded so unfamiliar to most Americans, so they would not get into trouble outside the base. In some cases, Americans would get a slap in the face if a Tagalog word was mispronounced. My American students reciprocated by teaching me the proper pronunciation of some English words.

In the Philippines, we all learned to speak English in elementary school. English is our second language. Until it was brought to my attention, I was not aware of my phonetic accent. Phonics was not stress in our school. We were taught a lot about spelling. I could correctly write down and spell a word used in a sentence, which was the standard practice in our English classes, but if I was just asked to pronounce a particular word, then I was not usually sure of its correct pronunciation. We just pronounced the English words however we thought they should sound, and we understood each other. We learned the meaning and the etymology of new words, but I had no clue that pronunciation made a lot of difference in the English language. The more I taught my students the Tagalog language, the more I discovered the similarities between the two languages. When a student mispronounced a word, it gave a different meaning to the word. I did not know that some words when mispronounced in the English language sound like bad words. I started to realize that I should make a good effort to pronounce my English words correctly.

One of my airmen student quietly took me aside one day and explained to me that my pronunciation of the word, "sheet" (piece) of paper sounded like "sh-t" (feces). I suddenly understood the frequent grins that I had seen on the faces of my students each time I mentioned "sheet of paper." To play it safe, I started using "piece of paper" as a substitute. It took me a while to pronounce it correctly. Oftentimes, when I am not paying attention, I still find myself mispronouncing the word, especially when I use it so many times in one day. There were a lot more words that, if mispronounced, took on a bad meaning, but I am not going to go on any further. Some are *really, really,* bad.

Introduction to Friendship

Mark, one of the military captains who took my class in Tagalog, had introduced me to his friend, Juan who was the squadron commander in his group. He was a nice, blonde air force first lieutenant officer who enrolled for two terms in my evening Tagalog class. After several months in the class, he asked me out to lunch, but I was so completely preoccupied with my job responsibilities that I did not really have time to acknowledge his invitation.

In my country's custom, a single woman is never allowed to spend time with a man alone. She always has to have a chaperone; be it a sister, a brother or a relative. However, a male suitor would be welcome to join a family gathering. In high school we all mingled in mixed groups of teenagers, but, together, a boy and a girl would never, never spend time alone. Our Filipino customs seemed in this way to conflict with American customs.

Juan was very patient. He was persistent enough to keep asking, so I agreed to have lunch with him. We went to the Kelly cafeteria across the street from my office. We talked about our jobs and families, and we discovered that we enjoyed each other's company. He coached baseball for the military and civilian personnel after his military duties. He invited me to attend their games and their after-the-game parties, and when I had a chance, I went to some of the gatherings. Soon I became a familiar part of their cheering group. Cheerleading was a natural role for me. My enthusiasm might have been modeled after my mother's spontaneous singing, and my family's boisterous gatherings upstairs at my aunt and uncle's house.

I missed my family, so I took a bus home every weekend to visit them in their new apartment in Manila. The first time that Juan visited and met my parents and family in Manila, my father was as uncommunicative as a concrete wall. He stared suspiciously at Juan from various angles of the room. My mother was more open to the idea of having an American guest as a suitor for her second daughter. She took my father aside to explain to him that Juan seemed to be a nice man who had a good job on the base. Of course, my father said nothing in response; he just stared blankly at the floor.

Patience Paved the Way

After a year of courtship, Juan visited my parents' apartment for the second time—this time to ask for their permission to marry me. He came to Manila by himself, driving his green *balut* (green jeep). A *balut* is a boiled duck egg fermented for several weeks and eaten with salt and pepper. Often times, they were eaten with beer. Juan invited my parents and fourteen relatives to a picnic in the Luneta Park, a popular public park, where we all watched the sunset. Sixteen of us were cramped like sausages and on top of each other in his nice, clean jeep. He was so patient and he did not mind at all. We were in the midst of throngs of people who had come out of their homes to mingle on a hot evening outside the city. The day was beautiful and Juan asked my father for my hand in marriage. My father stared at the ground and asked, "Will you take good care of Ning? Juan seriously responded, "Yes, sir." Then my father looked at my mother and said, with hesitation in his voice, looking at the ground again and nodding, "Okay."

My father spoke few words to Juan that evening in the park, but my grandmother liked him, and they had a lively conversation throughout the evening. As the sun began to set and the sky was streaked in brilliant orange and fuchsia, my father took me aside and quietly asked me if I was sure about marrying Juan. He whispered, "Are you sure you want to marry him? They have divorce in America, you know, and we may never see you again." With concern in his voice he added, "And who is going to take care of us?" Juan assured him that we would never get a divorce and bring shame on the family. I promised to continue to financially support them and pay for their expenses and school tuition. He was quiet for a long period of time while we all stared at him, waiting for an answer. Then, he hesitantly agreed to the wedding, and everyone grinned with relief and congratulated us and wished us a long, healthy life together.

The Wedding

My father was the most excited member of the family on my wedding day. He was dressed in his best formal white b*arong* Tagalog, a traditional white silk embroidered shirt worn by Filipino men for special occasions, with black slacks and his best shined and spotless leather shoes. He stood quietly with my mother in a cluster of relatives, smiling broadly. My mother looked beautiful and elegant in her long green silk embroidered *saya*, a silk dress with pointed sleeves which resemble the delicate wings of a butterfly.

Juan and I were married in a formal military wedding at Clark Air Force Base. We invited his entire squadron, my students and office personnel, and our friends and relatives. He was a first lieutenant in the air force, and he looked handsome in his formal white air force uniform jacket with its double-breasted gold buttons and epaulets, a bow-tie and black slacks. He was attended by six officer friends, who stood in rigid military salute. Our wedding was considered a very formal military wedding. In the Philippines, the groom pays for all the wedding expenses, including the wedding gown, reception and the honeymoon.

Ning's military wedding

I was attended by nine bridesmaids in bright pink silk embroidered dresses. My youngest sister, Shirley, was the flower girl, scattered rose petals down the aisle. My floor-length white satin wedding dress was embroidered with silk threads, sequins and, pearls, detailed at the bodice with a scalloped edge. Wearing a silk net veil and crowned by a rhinestone tiara, I felt like a princess. My mother whispered to me, with tears in her eyes, that I looked like a "shining star." *Luningning* means "shining star" in Tagalog.

After our wedding vows, my new husband and I walked together under a canopy of six swords held high with the blades crossed in the air to form a silver arch. Then my father proudly performed a ceremony where he released two white doves into the sky, symbolizing freedom, peace, and blessings for a long and healthy life.

He reached into the basket for the doves and symbolically threw them high into the air, but in the midst of all the excitement, he had forgotten to untie their legs. The birds were loosely bound together by their legs to hold them in place in the basket. The birds flew upwards in an awkward flight, and then fell to the ground in a thump of flapping wings. Everyone laughed, including my father, as he untied the birds and released them from his hands to fly smoothly, as originally planned, into the blue sky. It was a perfect day.

Our Honeymoon

We spent our honeymoon in John Haye Air Base, Baguio City, 50 miles north of Clark Air Force Base. It is the R&R (Rest and Recuperation) city for all the military personnel stationed in the Philippines. In fact, it is considered the" summer capital" of the Philippines. It was paradise to me. I had been there, in the Teacher's Camp during college conferences, but not for any vacation. It had roaring hills and pine trees, and the air was crisp and clean. We stayed in one of the military houses on the base there. It was so beautiful, with a fireplace and an exquisite hardwood floor covered with blue scattered rugs. I did not cook at all. We ate out for a week and tasted all the food and delicacies off and on base. We had a lot of quiet and romantic dinners during those seven days.

The honeymoon could not be real! My friends had told me that Juan and I would have some differences of opinion or a little quarrel. Guess what? We did. It happened on the third day. The base had a huge golf course, and Juan played golf. I went and walked with him. He had a caddy. I had never played golf before. The only knowledge I had of golf were the names Arnold Palmer and Jack Nicklaus, which I had seen as a child on newspapers pasted on our crawl space beams. I did not know any of the golf rules, and I did not know that I was supposed to be quiet when he was set to swing his clubs. Just as he was starting to swing his club, I talked loudly, and he shouted at me, "Will you please keep quiet!" Immediately my feelings got hurt. I did not talk to him for the rest of the game. He did not apologize until the end of the eighteenth hole. I felt so miserable. After that I did not want to play or be engaged in that sport. Eventually, however, I changed my mind. After thirty years, I tried playing the game and finally came to understand why I had to keep quiet at certain times.

Each morning, during our honeymoon, a young boy, named Cesar would pick us up and drive us around. We went shopping, eating, and sightseeing. I enjoyed shopping with Juan. He let me buy what I wanted, especially plant materials and native handicrafts that we could use around the house. We bought a lot of wood carvings, salad bowls, a chess set made of wood, candle holders and gifts to give away when we got back to Clark. It was a honeymoon to remember, except for that little incident in the golf course.

We moved off the base into a new apartment in a gated military community. We invited my parents for a visit. My mother and father arrived with my younger sister, Tessie, carrying a gift. My father had made a sturdy step stool for me, planed smooth and polished to a glossy finish. The stool helped me to reach the canned foods stored on the high shelves that were built for tall Americans. I appreciated his quiet, practical gift of love. They walked through our new apartment in wide-eyed surprise commenting, as they always did, on how much room we had in our apartment. Both my parents always looked up in amazement, as if the ceiling would lower on them again, and all the gifts of progress would have turn out to been but a dream.

> ## Food leaves a good impression of ones love and hospitality.

I remembered my mother's advice to me about my being a good wife. She had suggested that I should serve my husband by cooking the foods that he liked. All I knew how to cook were Filipino recipes. I didn't know how to cook American food at all, so I consulted with another officer's wife about how to cook American recipes. Mrs. Cappel suggested that I begin with something simple, like a grilled cheese sandwich. Later, she said that I should learn other dishes such as potato salad, tuna casserole, macaroni and cheese, hot dogs, fried chicken, and hamburgers.

"A grilled cheese sandwich is easy," she said. "All you do is heat the skillet until it's very hot, then add the butter, the bread and cheese, and heat it on both sides until the cheese melts and the bread turns brown."

I had never seen a grilled cheese sandwich before in my life, but I followed her instructions explicitly, in the exact order she had told me. I began with the hot pan and butter. I added the cheese, then the bread on top of the cheese. I never thought of using two slices of bread. I turned the one slice of bread over, but the cheese had already melted into a burnt glutinous clump. I proudly served my husband a black, one-sided sandwich burnt like a piece of charcoal. He ate it graciously. The next day, I told Mrs. Cappel about it, and we both laughed.

Juan was a captive victim to my food experimentation. He ate my grilled cheese until I finally got it right. I cooked him an assortment of odd-looking and soupy tasting casseroles and steaks that were either undercooked or burned. We finally decided that he should take care of cooking the steak. He knew better.

> ### Wisdom is learning from your own mistakes.

I learned from my own mistakes. Baking bread was another area of cooking where I tried but did not quite make it. The first bread I tried to bake ended up as hard as a rock. As a joke, we decided to throw it at the wall to see what would happen. Guess what? It was so hard that it did not even break! The second time that I made the same bread recipe; it was the saltiest bread that I had ever tasted because I did not measure the correct amount of salt. After many attempts, I discovered the easy way; I finally decided to use the Bisquick roll recipe. Juan was always patient during my cooking trials and both of us found humor in my awkward attempts at being a good American cook, and a good wife.

Before marriage, my life experience was focused on survival at home and in school. Until I became an officer's wife, there had been no reason to learn about the confusing rules of American military protocol. I wanted to uphold the standards and responsibilities of the position, so I bought an Emily Post's book on proper etiquette. I loved learning new subjects, so, with the same interest as with my university studies, I studied the placement of cocktail forks and five ways to fold a napkin.

The book showed a complicated illustration of how to set a table for a formal dinner party. The diagram showed a layout of multiple utensils in varying sizes in specific locations around the plates. In the crawl space, we just simply use two utensils to eat with—a fork and a spoon. Oftentimes, we ate with our fingers and used forks and spoons only for special occasions. Most of the time, utensils were stored in a tin can and used as serving spoons. My mother provided a communal bowl of water that was used for cleaning our hands both before and after. Our custom was appropriate in our home, but Emily Post clearly had a different opinion. She had soup and dinner spoons; salad, dessert and dinner forks; salad and dinner plates and several glasses for wine, liquor, and water. In the crawl space, a fork, a spoon, a plate and a glass for water were enough. After a while, the Emily Post table settings seemed more appealing to me.

Our first year of marriage was filled with work, sports games and social activities. When Juan received his order to move from the Philippines to Newark, Ohio, in the United States, the adjustments I had made during our first year had moderately prepared me for the move; but still the thought of leaving my family and my country left me deeply sad. Life had presented me with an opportunity to travel to my dreamworld, but I was not emotionally ready to go. I was overwhelmed with thoughts about losing my support system of relatives and friends, and I wondered how I would survive in a new culture without them.

To live freely is to endure some sacrifices.

My mother had taught me to be optimistic during the difficult periods of my life. The move to Ohio was an opportunity to practice her advice by remembering the positive influence that America had had on my family since my childhood. I remember learning how to read English from the American newspapers on our ceiling, which surrounded me with words. It was like living among the pages of an open book. America brought more than my father's favorite coffee into our lives. American generosity gave us hope.

I still wondered if America was like the images shown on television where comedy, beauty pageants and western cowboys combined in my imagination to create an extraordinary, bewildering world. My mother had formed her fantasy of American life mostly through the music on the radio. The ideal world she imagined was an exciting one where she thought Americans burst into song and dance during the course of their daily routines. American music so uplifted her spirit that, as she sang every morning, with her voice stridently cutting through the dark barriers of poverty into joy. She copied dresses from discarded fashion magazines, and hand-stitched fragments of cloth into dresses that she wore to portray herself as a prosperous and elegant woman.

Moving to America

Several months after my husband had received his transfer papers, and I had received my visa, we packed our belongings to move to the United States. I cried for days when I realized that I was leaving my country, my family, my friends, and my teachers, who had been the foundation of my life. I would miss Manila; the sunsets saturated with layers of brilliant colors, the picnics with my cousins at the Luneta park, the comfort of hearing the voices of my mother and father speaking to me in our Tagalog language. I worried about my father's health and my mother's responsibility to care for everyone in my family. I had wondered how I would handle the changes of a new culture without the safety net of my family. I promised them that I would return for a visit once I got settled into our new home. I hugged them tight with tears flowing from my eyes and I told them, "You will always be in my heart."

The move from the Philippines to America nearly tore me apart. The opportunities that I had worked so hard to pursue with my mother's encouragement were separating us. My husband and I left my family in Manila, with their blessings to us for a happy and prosperous life across the globe. I didn't know what to expect in America, but I had hoped to see Lucille Ball.

Chapter 7

LIFE IN AMERICA

Lesson Seven: Be grateful for all that life has to offer.

On May 28, 1970, I took my first long international plane trip outside the Philippines. It was an exciting seventeen-hour flight. Soon after we were buckled into our seats, the flight attendants, who stood at stations along the long aisles of the airplane, asked for our attention over the loudspeaker. The sound coming out of the microphone distorted the flight attendant's voice making it hard for me to hear and understand her emergency instructions. The flight attendants, who were still called "stewardesses" in the seventies, looked like movie stars, dressed in identical pink uniforms with mini skirts. They pointed to the emergency exits and demonstrated the use of an oxygen mask through a mechanical routine of hand and arm gestures.

I wondered what my parents would think about the meals served on the jet. All passengers were served a perfect meal on white plastic oval plates. The portions of meat and vegetables were identical, and were magically cooked while flying in the air.

The seventeen-hour international flight seemed to last forever. I had plenty of time to read a book, sleep, eat, cry, read another book, and walk up and down the aisles of the plane to stretch. I wrote a poem for my mother, and then I read some more. I had finally prepared myself to go to America but was afraid the airplane would run out of fuel and we would crash into the ocean if I took a short nap. I regretted not listening more carefully to the garbled emergency instructions from the flight attendants.

Our port of entry into the United States was through Anchorage, Alaska where I experienced the feeling of being very cold for the first time in my life. We stood in a long line of people, had our documents checked, and then boarded another plane for our first destination, San Mateo, California, to visit Juan's favorite aunt, Hazel, and her family. We visited for a week. We felt jet-lagged, our nights became our days, and our days became our nights. We were wide-awake during the nights, and can't keep awake during the days. It took approximately a week to resume our normal sleeping habits. His Aunt Hazel's family was so warm and hospitable to me and I was received very well. We hugged, sang, and told stories, and we toured around the area and had hamburgers at McDonald's. After a week, we bid his family good-bye. I cried again, because I was leaving another very nice family and felt sad that we might not see them again. This brought back memories of my own family that I had left behind in the Philippines.

The next morning, we boarded a long, air-conditioned Greyhound bus which looked gigantic to me. It was so roomy, with even a built-in bathroom and a lot of spacious seats. Compared to our Philippine PanTranco buses so overcrowded with passengers and falling apart from constant use twenty-four hours a day, the Greyhound bus was a luxury coach.

We arrived in Oregon the following morning and picked up a brand new green 1970 Camaro from the car dealership. I could not comprehend what was going on at first. Juan was very excited about the new car. He acted like a little boy in a candy store—wide-eyed, happy and overjoyed. In the meantime, I was a little bit hesitant. His energy level was in high gear as he drove his brand-new car and headed to Seattle, where he was from. I was a bit worried that I might not be well received by his mother. The three hour drive seemed short. We talked a lot about his family, and he reassured me that his mom would like me.

Mother-in-Law

We finally arrived in Seattle. He hugged his mother. Right away, I felt some distance from her. I was cordial and smiling as Juan introduced me to her. Unfortunately, she did not seem to feel comfortable with me. I didn't think that I met her expectations. I was a quiet, dark, short Filipina with a very long black hair wound up in a bun, who looked a little malnourished and only weighed eighty-five pounds. All this time, I couldn't help but think of my family in the Philippines. I wondered what they were doing. For a brief moment, I had tears in my eyes. Suddenly, I heard my father's voice telling me not to shed any tears in public because to him that meant weakness and defeat. So then I quickly gained my composure and refocused my attention on my husband. I wanted to show him that he could be proud of me and that I was a good wife to him. I wanted us to enjoy our short visit with his family and his best friend and favorite cousin, Jerry, in Seattle. The purpose of the trip was really for him to enjoy his family and friends before we headed to the air force base in Ohio. As for me, I accepted his mother the way she was. Our differences would not change my love for his son and the American people. I could not allow one person to tarnish my faith and trust in America. The American people had given me the educational, financial and moral support that I now enjoy. I had hoped and prayed that someday I would be given a chance to serve and give something in return for their kindness and generosity that had been bestowed upon me.

Life in Ohio

After a month of homecoming visits, we drove to Ohio in our brand new car—the kind of car I never thought I would own. I was so overwhelmed by what was going on. I never realized how big America was—huge freeways, and days and days of driving from Seattle to Ohio. While he was driving, I would get flashbacks of memories and advice from my grandmother. She had told me to take good care of my husband, to be of good cheer, and to stay positive. Then she said, "Don't forget us. Write us soon." I started crying while my husband was driving and he knew I missed my family, so he reached over and touched my hand to comfort me.

> **Share what you have gained from your life's journey so that others may learn from it.**

We moved into a quiet, spacious three-bedroom house in the country side of Newark, Ohio. Unlike outside our crawl space home in the Philippines, I had plenty of room for a vegetable and flower garden. Our new home had a big open backyard with no hollow block walls separating houses and factories. Our home was filled with our new teak furniture which we had ordered from Taiwan, where we had vacationed just before moving to America. I was already feeling the big changes that were happening right before my eyes. The stack of boxes that contained our belongings was quickly unpacked by the movers and organized into our new home.

Each box that I had unpacked contained a memory that reminded me of my family. As a gift, my father had given me a tiny, gold-colored metal key that had once fit the lock of a suitcase. He had had no wrapping paper to wrap the gift, so the key had been passed from his hand to mine with a gentle smile as a token of his love. Packed next to the gold key was a gift from my mother. She had given me a manicure set, which had been given to her by her mother, which contained a nail file and a small pair of metal cuticle scissors wrapped in a piece of Manila paper. My brother had given me a woven grass mat for sleeping on the floor, and my younger sister, Lina, had crocheted a beautiful white bedspread with a deli-cate scalloped edge as our wedding present. I held the small key in the palm of my hand, and cried in silence.

> **The true test of love is how much we are willing to sacrifice for each other.**

There was so much to learn about living in a modern home. One of my challenges was to try to use several kinds of electrical appliances. I had seen pictures of a vacuum cleaner in magazines, but had never used one. At Clark Air Base, the bungalow in the Hill Hacienda had beautiful golden hardwood floors that the housekeeper swept clean with a palm broom (*walis*). When Juan and I were married and lived in an apartment, our housekeeper meticulously swept the linoleum floors to sheen. However, our home on Randy Drive on the outskirts of Newark, Ohio, had a large living room, three bedrooms and hallways that were all covered with wall-to-wall blue carpeting. To me, it looked like acres of carpeting and a vacuum cleaner was essential.

First Encounter of the Fourth Kind

My first encounter with a vacuum cleaner was very frightening and proved to be a bit hazardous. My husband told me to plug the vacuum into the electric outlet by the wall and just go over the whole floor. I did as I was told and I vacuumed everything in sight—his socks, staples, small pieces of paper left from unpacking the boxes, his handkerchiefs, and his underwear. I was having fun, singing as I went along until I heard a loud noise and smoke coming out of the motor. "Oh my goodness, it overheated." The house was suddenly filled with smoke and smelled like burned rubber. I urgently called him at his office. I was holding the phone, shaking and jumping with fright, not knowing what to do or what had had happened. When his secretary gave him my call, by getting him out of a staff meeting, he spoke to me calmly and gave me instructions to just go ahead and unplug the electrical cord from the wall outlet, open all the windows, and not to worry. He said that he would be home right after his meeting. I felt better after he reassured me that everything was going to be all right.

> Have patience. Success is a process of trial and error.

Over the weeks and months that followed, I continued to learn by trial and error. Using the toaster, washer, dryer, and garbage disposal were equally confusing. I put bleached in with colors, burned bread in the toaster, and overloaded the garbage disposal. I had learned not to be startled by the sound of the toast suddenly popping up out of the toaster. I learned that when you put too much bleach into the washing machine, it puts holes in your clothes, or dissolves them, or turns the colors white. I eventually learned how to separate colors from whites. I also learned that chicken bones make a terrible sound when they're being ground up in the garbage disposal, and they also cause the disposal to quit working. You would think that all these mistakes were enough to make my husband mad. But no, he remained calm, cool, and collected. After a while I learned and succeeded in operating all our appliances.

Period of Adjustment

As an immigrant, with so much to learn, I tried very hard to blend into the American culture. Flexibility had always been an important attitude for survival throughout my life. As an immigrant, it was essential. I had noticed that many of the rules were different. For instance, I had noticed that the United States had clearly defined rules of conduct for driving.

In Manila, speed limits and traffic signals were seldom followed. Drivers bravely faced a chaotic rush of freight trucks, jeepneys and motor scooters which all battled for the same space on the road. Very few signs were posted on the roads, forcing drivers to guess the distance from one city to the next. Drivers would suddenly swerve off the main road onto a side road, dodging people, pushing carts with caged chickens and other pedestrians.

With this memory of chaotic driving still fresh in my mind, I was hesitant to learn how to drive, even in America, where driving conditions were much safer than in Manila. But I knew that driving a car was a necessity when living miles away from everything, especially from shopping centers. I decided that I'd better learn how to drive so that I wouldn't have to wait for my husband to drive me around. After a month of cleaning and organizing our new home, getting a driver's license was my next step in becoming an independent wife in America.

I have always learned new skills through very specific verbal instruction, and learning to drive was no exception to this rule. My first driving lesson was startling. I got nervous taking lessons from my husband, so I enrolled in a driving school. One Saturday, I drove around, with my instructor sitting on the passenger side. I was having fun, just getting to know the road and staying between the lines. I felt comfortable. After my first lesson, still in the school parking lot, my husband was so proud of me that he had me drive our brand-new, automatic, 1970 Camaro. He convinced me that if I could drive between the lines, I could put the car in reverse with no problem and back up. I took over the driver's seat and he nicely told me to put the transmission lever on "R." I slowly put the car in reverse and steped on the gas. I did exactly what he told me. I reversed, and stepped on the gas. Suddenly, we heard a big *boom,* a loud *bang* and a squeaky rubbing of metal. My head jolted forward, and I backed directly into the front of my driving instructor's car. My instructor was sitting in his car filling in his report for that day, when he felt the heavy jolt. I saw his eyes widened and he was shaken, too, although he acted calmly. My husband had forgotten to tell me to look in the rear view mirror to make sure that everything was clear and then going easy on the gas pedal so that I would have more control while backing up the car. I should have known better. That was the first lesson that my driving instructor taught me—to make all the adjustments and to look in the rearview mirror to check for cars behind me. I had had my first car accident.

This mistake left me in tears, trembling, shook up, and frustrated. That very moment, I wanted to return back home, to Manila, where life was simpler. Both instructor and my husband tried to talk me into finishing my lessons. A few days later, I did return to the driving class, and I then learned more about the complexities of safe driving. After several weeks of driving, I took a driving test for the first time in my life. I passed and received my driver's license. I was thrilled. That very moment, I discovered a new type of freedom that I had never experienced before. I was able to drive and go shopping by myself. I was able to drive by myself to the public library and check out books. I finally got to read a lot of "how-to" books—how to cook, how to clean, and how to garden. This new-found-love kept me happy and busy, instead of being alone in our apartment while my husband was at work. I felt happy and on top of the world.

I also found time to drive to church to pray for my family. I enjoyed my newfound freedom. I started attending the Officers' Wives' Club meetings, having lunch with friends, and getting to know more about the Officers' Wives' functions and activities. I was constantly amazed, and was deeply grateful for the way that my new world had started to unfold.

We settled comfortably into our home in the countryside, where I planted a small garden in the backyard, with orderly rows of onions, lettuce, tomatoes and carrots. Pink cosmos, my mother's favorite flower, filled the clay pots next to our entry. Each time I cut a bouquet of cosmos for the dining room table, I thought of her.

> **God's blessings are always present in the garden.**

We began to fulfill our promise to my parents to help ease their financial burden. We sent money to my family each month and gift packages to them every Christmas. The packages contained items such as their favorite brand of coffee, towels, and tools for my father, clothing, toys and cosmetics for my brothers and sisters, and a brand new toaster for my mom. I sent them used wrapping paper as a gift, knowing that a new roll would never be used; thrift continued to be a way of life for my parents.

Gift of Life

At sunrise, on a clear, crisp December morning in 1971, Juan and I welcomed the birth of our first daughter, Maria. She was a beautiful baby girl with soft black hair. She looked like an angel in red, wrapped in a white cotton blanket. Maria was our Christmas present. After I had been in labor for twenty-three hours, Juan was so proud of being a new father. He stood tall with his back straight, and handed out cigars to everyone. We both shared the joy of the birth of our daughter. When she was born, the first thing I thought of was my mother. She would have loved to see Maria being born.

My mother was present at Maria's birth, in my heart. It was she who taught me, and my sisters, about the customs surrounding childbirth and motherhood. As a young girl, I watched my mother and aunts gather to support female relatives during and after child birth. As their own mothers had done for generations before them, they would tell the new mother to rest and stay in bed and all the relatives would attend to all her needs. Each woman would share their stories about her own experiences of labor and birth. In this way, they would show their love and respect for all women in the celebration and the miracle of life. This fellowship of women was a tradition passed through generations of daughters. Often, the first meal that was prepared for the new mother after birth was rice noodles called *pansit*. But the true nourishment was love and companionship.

During my own delivery, I missed hearing my mother's confident, soothing voice telling me that everything would be all right. The tradition of being attended to by my mother, sisters and aunts was not meant to be; however, I was comforted by my husband, who shared his joy in the birth of our daughter. In place of the Philippine noodle, he brought me some spaghetti, which closely resembles *pansit* noodles.

> ## Joy shared with loved ones will always be cherished.

A Dream Come True

When Maria was about three months old, I felt ready to pursue my dream of becoming a teacher in America. I went to Denison University, a vicinity of Granville, Ohio, close to where we lived. I met with the dean, who reviewed all my documents and transcripts from the Philippines. I was worried that I might have to go back to school before I could be issued my teaching certificate. After the final review, I was informed that my credits were more than enough to be issued a teaching certificate in the state of Ohio. When I received my teaching certificate in a brown envelope in the mail, I balanced Maria on my left hip and spun around in a little celebration dance at the mailbox. Another dream had become a reality.

I framed my teaching certificate, and kissed it, and held it to my heart. That day at the mailbox was a special day of celebration for my parents and my teachers. My success was theirs. I had promised my mother and father that I would share the gift of education with my students whose struggles were similar to mine, and with whom I would share my deepest compassion.

I thought about the many times when I was a child, when I had pretended to be a teacher. I would gather my brothers, sisters, and the neighbor children in the alley across from our house to teach the alphabet. The neighbor's concrete wall became a chalkboard where I taught my "students" how to form the letters of the alphabet. I used discarded pieces of chalks that had been given to me by my teacher as a reward for assisting and being a "big sister" in the classroom.

> **To teach is to extend your given gifts in the presence of God.**

My initial plan to become a teacher had taken a different route when I accepted my first job as an assistant chief financial officer in Clark Air Force Base. But with my newly acquired teaching certificate, I was back on a track for which I felt the greatest satisfaction and purpose.

I received a telephone call that I had been accepted for a teaching position at the Green Joint Vocational and Technical College, a community college in Xenia, Ohio. This job was to teach three, one-hour blocks of evening classes. It worked out. I could be with my baby daughter, Maria, during the day and my husband could attend to her during the night. The part-time position was a short drive from our home. I taught typing, business management and distributive education, also known as marketing.

I had a passion to teach typing, which was a skill I had learned in high school that represented a personal triumph. I remembered vividly, as a young student, when my typing teacher had told me in class that I would never be able to type because I had double-jointed fingers, which to her was a form of disability. This handicap, to her, would make it impossible for me to manipulate the keys of a typewriter. Her sad remarks taught me a powerful lesson about the a teacher's important responsibility to encourage students to reach for their dreams and their potentials, regardless of their disabilities.

Years later while attending college, I entered a typing competition and won the Champion Typist Award for Speed Typing. Most of all, I carried an important lesson from this experience in my typing class. I made a promise to myself that, when I became a teacher that I would support and encourage each of my students to dig deeper inside into their unique potential. I would teach them not to limit themselves of their disabilities..

> ## Nobody is perfect. Think of the many possibilities compared to the few impossibilities.

My first experience as a teacher in America was ideal. The staff and students were gracious and helpful on my first day of class. The campus was brand-new, and all the electronic equipments were "state-of-the-art." Classes began with the introductions—the students said their names, and I told the joke that if they could pronounce my full name, Maria Luningning Julian Buenaventura Samson Frasier, by the end of the term, then they would pass.

The Tornado

A few months into my evening classes, the students were concentrating on their assignments when the lights in the classroom suddenly began to flicker on and off. Without warning, the college was shaken by an extraordinary force that ripped through the campus. Everyone in the classroom was startled by a deafening sound that I later learned was the vibration from one of the strongest tornadoes ever recorded in Xenia, Ohio. The winds slammed into the campus and hurled metal beams through the air, ripped out trees by their roots, and shifted concrete walls. Most of the students knew how to react in that kind of an emergency and they told me to crawl under a desk until the loud vibrations subsided. The powerful wind funnel destroyed half the campus, but, remarkably our classroom was spared.

Everything was new to me in America. I had not yet developed survival instincts about the dangers in my new environment, nor had I even known that there were dangers. In the Philippines, an approaching typhoon was predicted through the senses: The humidity in the atmosphere would intensify and cling heavily to our bodies. The sky would shift quickly in color from clear blue to an intense blackish gray. Animal sounds would become sharp and agitated; the chickens and ducks would dart through the house as if chased by an invisible broom.

Until that dramatic experience on campus, I had never known what a tornado was, and so I did not know how to respond to it. It was different in the Philippines when I lived with the animals under the house and was attuned to the changes in their behavior. I also felt the shifts in the atmosphere when I lived there. But in Ohio, earlier in the day of the tornado, I hadn't noticed the greenish tint of the sky, which signaled an impending storm. I had been focused only on teaching typing on the sleek, new electric typewriters, whose keys glided with an effortless hum. The powerful tonado confirmed that the cycle of destruction and reconstruction, which oftentimes was common in my life, was still present even in America.

Life in Dayton

My husband, our daughter, Maria and I had spent two years living in Newark, Ohio, where I was always been grateful for the kindness of my colleagues, students, neighbors, and friends. It was them who generously taught me about life in the United States and prepared me for our next assignment.

Our new ranch-style home was outside the city of Dayton, in the countryside, but not far from the city. Its hardy cedar siding was painted deep moss green and was bordered from the bottom edge of the windows to the ground by a brick facade. A metal chain-link fence, covered abundantly by fragrant, red rambling roses, surrounded the house. The inside entrance of our new home, to me, was gigantic. The rotating waterwheel in the foyer dipped rhythmically into a recycled channel of water and gave a soothing welcome. When I first stood in our new entry, I realized that the entrance of this house was larger than my family's entire living space in Manila. I couldn't help comparing my past to my present life.

> **More grows in the garden than the gardener sows.**
> **Spanish proverb**

Gardening in Ohio fulfilled my desire to be connected to God's abundant earth. I planted a colorful mixture of onions, petunias and marigolds at the base of the rose-covered fence in the backyard. My vegetable garden was filled with tomatoes, onions, cucumbers, zucchini, cauliflower and cabbage planted in rich soil that had produced a robust harvest.

Hoeing long furrows of warm, rich soil, planting seeds, and watching them grow, nourished my soul.

Juan, Maria, and I had settled comfortably into the ranch house. Because of my new life, my mother in the Philippines was afraid that I might forget about my family back home. She never realized how much their love and influence held me in place like a deep root, anchoring me during many personal storms. I often thought about my family and hoped that they, too, were content in their lives. They, with extraordinary appreciation, accepted their clean water, adequate, food and comfortable home—luxuries that many of us in America took for granted.

Preparing for Citizenship

My next goal was to prepare for my American citizenship. Once a week for three months, I drove a short distance to Columbus, Ohio to join other men and women who gathered at the YMCA building for citizenship classes. Immigrants from the Philippines, Germany, Mexico, Japan, China and other countries studied American history, government, and local and national current events, I was excited to meet a

Filipino woman for the first time, since I had come to the United States. We spoke to each other about our country in Tagalog, which left us both feeling nostalgic for our native land.

The day I received my American citizenship in Columbus, Ohio, was a memorable occasion. All the immigrants who took the tests awaited the results of the two-hour written and oral exam we had taken. The excitement we felt was also counterbalanced by the sadness of giving up our citizenship to become Americans. As I waited for the test results, I thought about my mother's encouragement and the sacrifices that she had made for me to pursue education and ultimately move to America.

My husband and our friends, Dave and Mitch, who served as my witnesses, were present for the ceremony. All the newly pledged Americans and their families celebrated the occasion with hugs and handshakes.

I was pregnant with our second child, during that time, and I felt honored to know that my children would receive the gifts of opportunity that my own family, in the Philippines had not had. Juan took us for a celebration dinner at our favorite Italian restaurant. We had developed a tradition to have spaghetti, instead of the *pansit*. Since spaghetti noodles are more readily available than the pancit noodles in restaurants and supermarkets, we began serving it in many of our celebrations, like my citizenship party. In the Philippines, *pancit* were often times served because it means "long life".

To Be an American

Citizenship poem by Ning Samson

1973

Here I am in the land of the free,

A life time dream of mine—a life time dream of many.

The nation of abundance and many opportunities,

An immigrant's dream finally came to reality.

Here I am—so blessed and honored

In the land of the free and the land of the plenty,

I feel like an eagle flying up-up so high,

My wings so stretched out, soaring up in the sky.

"I pledge allegiance to the flag of the United States of

America"

Are the exact words I said,

To this great nation that gave me

All the wisdom that I now have.

Here I am, Lord, to spread your joy and peace

To the citizens of this country who made me feel at ease.

I promise to educate and give back what I have gained

To this loving country, on whose people I can depend.

On this day when I was sworn, my allegiance and faith,

America, the beautiful, the greatest nation on earth,

I will serve and uphold the law of the land,

I will be among the gracious, and proud *to be an American.*

Mother's Arrival in the United States

Our second daughter, Juliann, was born on a hot August day in 1973. She was warmly welcomed by her father, her older sister, Maria and me. In the winter of the same year, my mother moved from Manila, Philippines, to live with us to help us care for our children. After our relatives assured my mother that they would all help my father with the house chores and take care of him, then she decided to travel and sacrifice for our sake.

Mother arrived at O'Hare International Airport in Chicago with few belongings in her old cardboard luggage. When I saw her coming out of the airplane door, I could not help but smile and cry with tears in my eyes. We both cried as we kissed and gave each other a big and a long welcome hug. This time, crying meant love and not defeat as my father would say. Juan was holding our two small children, Maria and Juliann, while she gave him a big, big hug and kissed both our sleeping angels. We loaded her only carry-on worn and old suitcase box into our car. It was a cold and a snowy winter night. She looked up in the sky, shivered, and asked, "Why is the white rain so cold?" I replied, "Mom, you are seeing snow and not rain. This is your first snow."

> **There is no greater sacrifice than a mother's love for her child.**

Having to sacrifice was in my mother's blood and bone. In accepting our call for help, she gave us the unselfish devotion she had demonstrated throughout her lifetime. Her strength was born of love and fortified by a compassionate, steadfast faith. She had quietly entered into our lives, and blended seamlessly into our family. Her presence was comforting and very familiar to me. Her help with cooking, cleaning, and watching the children was invaluable to us.

My mother's influence on our children helped them connect with their roots and heritage. She spoke only Tagalog to them, and cooked some traditional foods, like *pancit* and *adobo*. She brought her knowledge of herbal healing, where she healed Maria's scraped knee with the gel from an aloe vera plant as she had done for me when I was growing up. She was our natural healer.

While living and teaching on the air force base in the Philippines, I had the advantage of learning about the American culture in small increments. On the contrary, my mother did not have that advantage. The changes for her were monumental. I will never forget my mother's reaction the very first time I took her shopping at Hancock fabric store. In the Philippines, fabric was touched only when purchased. In America, she could not believe that she could touch fine silks and satins embroidered with pearls to her hearts content. She stood in silence, observing the rows of hundreds of perfect bolts of brightly patterned materials. Her head turned slowly, absorbing hundreds of hues and colors from every aisle and corner of the fabric store. Circular kiosks of fabric surrounded and towered over her. Ribbons and spools of thread were as bright as the sunsets in the Philippines, and some were as iridescent as the feathers of the roosters that had walked so freely through our crawl space. Mother thought the excessive amount of material could surely clothe the whole world.

Chapter 8

A TEACHER'S DREAM

Lesson Eight: You will become what you believe.

Move to the Pacific Northwest

$\mathcal{M}$y husband had acquired employment in the Pacific Northwest. In the meantime, we all stayed temporarily with his mother while we looked for a house to live. We began work almost immediately. My first teaching job in Seattle, Washington was at Nathan Hale High School with the Seattle school district. The school was built in the sixties of red brick, and a tall, boiler room smokestack that protruded high into the air was its most distinguishing feature. The neighborhood surrounding the school had modest homes nestled between tall spruce and fir trees. The students who attended my business classes were from predominantly middle-class families.

Most of the students had a supportive environment for their education at home, resulting in students who were motivated to succeed in class and in life.

At Nathan Hale, I taught business education classes: accounting, marketing/distributive education, typing, (later called keyboarding), business law, finance and graphic arts. I had three spacious class rooms. One room was specifically designed for accounting, another for marketing/distributive education, and the third room was for my typing classes. My marketing/distributive education students operated the school store, which gave them the opportunity to practice their salesmanship and business management skills they had learned in class. Students in training arrived in the early morning—an hour before class—to open the store. In the store, students practiced salesmanship skills and public relations, while selling soda pop, shirts, hats, candy, and school supplies. They learned how to use the cash registers and were responsible for purchasing, and taking stock of the inventory that they had ordered. To teach the students the value of contribution, a percentage of their profits were given to our school student fund.

Personal and Ethical Values

A portion of my class discussion was to talk about the importance of responsibility and honesty in business. I reminded my students that personal ethics, which included responsibility and honesty, are valuable qualities that form the heart of one's character, and remain with a person for a lifetime. An individual whose life reflects the daily use of strong ethical values will always be an important asset to any kind of business. This kind of worker will inspire his or her coworkers to strive for excellence.

I told them about my business philosophy: that when passion for customer service is pursued as a primary goal instead of greed and big profits, then business owners will be contented and happier with their private lives, and consequently with their business. Only then will financial success follow them throughout their business careers. When you pursue your passions of serving customers in any kind of business, money will follow. Every student seemed excited by the idea that they could create a business around something they enjoyed. Until then, most of them believed that making money was the only object for being in business.

Financial success could also be a powerful tool to help individuals and the community. When money is contributed to helping others, this generosity increases the personal satisfaction of the giver. That was my father's guiding principle, but he could give only beautiful boxes instead of money.

> **A child's life is like a piece of paper on which every person leaves a mark.** Chinese proverb

The Importance of College Education

Several students had asked me about my thoughts on the importance of a college education. In my life in the Philippines, a college education had been vital. The skills I had learned in college had qualified me for a dream job, when hundreds of other applicants were competing for the same job. Education was the only tool available that would help improve my life and the life of my family. Although a college education is indeed a valuable tool, it is only one ingredient in the "soup." There are many paths and methods for achieving success. College is not for every one but it is a vital ingredient in today's world where our country is continually competing in today's global market. College education is now necessary and must be encourage by parents, teachers, and counselors if we have to remain the best and the wealthiest nation on earth.

A college education may not be the right choice for everyone but nevertheless one must choose an education beyond high school so they can someday support a family. I tell my students often enough to not be satisfied in working for minimum wage. They must possess a certain drive to continue learning and reach for the impossible. The most important quality is to have the desire to pursue an idea with enthusiasm and persistence. I believe that successful people usually posses the qualities of ambition, personal responsibility, determination, resourcefulness, punctuality, honesty and common sense, but not necessarily a college degree.

The point I wanted to bring up in my discussion would be to support the students whose ideas were exciting, but who nonetheless struggled academically in school. Those students had a look of relief on their faces. They told me that they felt hopeful that other options were open to them, and that their ideas were valued. My first years at Nathan Hale concluded with the satisfaction that I had tried my best to listen, help direct, and support my students.

> **To teach is to be compassionate.**

Because of staff cutbacks in the whole Seattle school district that year and with my lowest rank in seniority, I found myself without a job the following year. However, shortly thereafter, I received a call for a teaching position at Mount Baker Youth Service Bureau, an alternative school in south Seattle, still within the Seattle school district. I had been recommended to the principal to teach business and typing classes. I was then, shortly after, invited to visit the school for an interview.

The Alternative High School was in a building that had been a chain grocery store. It was cold, dreary, and dark. During my interview for the position, the principal asked me repeatedly if I was certain about wanting the job, as though he felt I hadn't grasped the difficult nature of the teaching position. I assured the principal, Mr. Gary Little, that the job would be a great opportunity for me to teach and help the type of students who needed some directions and guidance not only in school, but also in his or her personal life. I told the principal that I wanted to help these students by giving them the respect they deserved as individuals and by directing their paths so they might have a chance for a better future. If I could make a difference in even one student's life, I would think that I had succeeded. That very same day, Mr. Little told me that I could have the position. I gladly accepted the assignment.

A Teacher and a Mentor

My teachers in the Philippines had taught me about the powerful influence of a mentor. A mentor inspires students to reach their inner potentials. Mentors have affected my life many times. I had hoped that my faith in students' talents would be a catalyst in helping them to believe in themselves. I wanted my classes to have an effect similar to drops of water dripping on a rock for a millennium, opening the minds and hearts of a few students. But I knew I didn't have a millennium. I only had a limited amount of time in their rapidly changing lives to present this opportunity for enrichment. Like a drop of water on a rock, a student's few semester of positive experience from me as their teacher and mentor can mean a lifetime of positive living and success in their future.

> **Education can be an important tool for changing the world around us.**

Hope for a Better Life

Standing slight four-feet, nine inches tall and pregnant, I must have appeared fragile and out of place to my streetwise teenage students who towered above me. I became accustomed to the jokes about my "stunted growth" in reference to my growing up in the cramped crawl space in my country. However, the students did recognize my sincere commitment to their individual struggles and my desire to support them for a bright and successful future.

As our mutual trust developed, some students revealed the painful nature of their lives and privately shared a glimpse of their dreams. These young adults were clearly afraid to hope for better lives. Some students whispered their goals to me, with their backs turned away from the other students in the class, as if to block out the dark force of ridicule.

I often brought a large box of glazed doughnuts, milk and juice to school before the class started. The students would jolt awake when they saw the box of pastries in the classroom, and they were grateful for the food before starting the tedious work in accounting. While they ate, I would tell them stories about my childhood. I asked them to try and imagine cooking pastries on a coffee tin stove instead of having the convenience of buying them from a bakery.

Some students slouch in their chairs, seeming sleepy and completely disinterested in the descriptions of my life struggles in the Philippines. Others would listen with compassion and try to understand, gaining a new appre-

Coffee tin stove used to cook

ciation of the strength and the will that is necessary for immigrants to improve their lives. What was true for me was also true for them. I hoped that the stories of harsh survival would help them to appreciate the security and conveniences they had in their own country.

Both my adult college students in Ohio and my teenage high school students in Seattle believed that "abundance," meant the act of acquiring possessions. They both felt that their individual importance and values were measured only by material possessions. I wanted to change their perception by helping them realize that they possessed their own abundance within themselves. I wanted them to realize that their self-esteem would show through after they realized and believed this.

While teaching my accounting class, I also spoke to the students about the importance of self-respect. I absolutely believed that cynical attitudes and negative assumptions about themselves could be replaced with hope. I spoke about the fact that perceived limitations were often the most difficult obstacles to overcome in oneself. If people think that they cannot do something, then they limit themselves, and they stop making an effort to succeed. People who feel good about themselves also treat others with respect, and that is fundamentally important.

A majority of my students in the Alternative School received little or no support from their parents and families. Their parents and families seemed to have a lot more challenges beyond attending to their children. The students showed the effects of abuse and neglect by their destructive behaviors and negative attitudes which oftentimes prevented them from even trying their best. These important factors limited them from being a better person.

I also talked to them about the deeper, human aspects of the spirit. I read them inspirational quotes and passages from my own life experiences and from the many spiritual books I have read throughout the years, hoping that maybe, these ideas might open their hearts and give way to a new spirit. I told them that they had to remain strong, to be able to rise above and beyond their feeling of despair and their oppressive circumstances. The choice was theirs and I let them know that I was available to help them.

> Don't let the past poison your future. Let your setbacks be stepping stones for tomorrow's challenges.

When students slept at their desks or stared blankly at the wall, I told them that I knew that they didn't want to be in school, but I was proud of them for coming. Education, I said, was a gift not granted to millions of people in the third world and poor countries, like the Philippines. They were so blessed that education was available to them. I kept reminding them that they were all special and blessed, and that they all had been given some kind of gift to share with the world. They have to find it within themselves. My job as their teacher was to help them find their talents deep inside—the gifts that God had given them from the time they were born. I promised to try to help them learn the practical life survival skills that they would need to accomplish their goals. As always, I told them that a clear vision and passion for what they wanted to accomplish in life was more important than a college education. Through hard work and persistence, their ideas and dreams could be spun into gold.

> **Every success starts with a dream. Take a hold of it. It will someday come true.**

A Transformation

The transformation in some of my students was a privilege to cherish. I remember the day when a beautiful young girl named Samantha, who worked as a teenage prostitute, asked me to help her prepare for another job. She wanted to be a secretary. This kind of opportunity—to teach "in the eye of the storm"—was the very thing that I had been preparing for all my life.

By the end of the year, the young woman had met my strict requirement of 100 percent attendance. I remember, during one winter snowstorm, when road conditions were dangerous, she still came to class with her completed assignments and was the only student present. As days and weeks went by, her classmates began to regard her as a role model as they saw her developed a good self-image. She worked so hard so she could finish school.

> **Teachers open the door, but you must enter through it yourself.** Chinese proverb

On the last day of school, I kept my promise to take that student out to her "dream" restaurant. Her dream was to have lunch in the elegant and famous, revolving restaurant on top of the Space Needle in Seattle. Her confidence was evident in her posture as she walked into the classroom that morning. She stood tall, dressed discreetly in a blue suit jacket and skirt with a white blouse, and black leather shoes.

When the elevator took us up to the top of the Space Needle, she stood quietly in awe of the panoramic view of Seattle. This was the view she'd been waiting to see for all those years while she was growing up. She had told me, "Someday, I will be able to eat up in the Space Needle." We both hugged each other and we both started to cry. I told her about the hardships and the challenges I had gone through just to be able to go to school in the Philippines when I was young. She had emerged from the shadow of a destructive life to find her own strengths and values. I felt privileged to watch as her hard work and commitment turned into success—her dream to make a better life had come true. I was so glad to be a part of her life.

One cycle was complete; my teachers in the Philippines had believed in me, and I believed in her. God was alive in the exchange of giving and receiving the gifts of hope and encouragement.

Chapter 9

TRIALS IN LIFE

Lesson Nine: Life is filled with unexpected turns. We have to follow the winding roads before we can make a breakthrough.

My Only Boy

Shortly after the end of the school year at Mt. Baker Youth Service Bureau, our third child, Edward, was born on a hot summer day in August. This was a proud occasion for me and my husband. Juan called his family and coworkers to announce the birth of his first and only son. My daughters anxiously awaited our homecoming to meet their new brother. My mother was in America for the birth of her grandson. She held him gently, the same way she had held all of us, her seven children, when we were born. She had tears in her eyes. Her presence was as comforting as my being cradled in her arms.

Our household was complete. Edward was a handsome little boy, wearing a tiny blue baseball hat on his head the very first hour of his life. He was a happy boy. He and his two sisters, Maria, and Juliann, were all happy as babies—always smiling and peaceful.

My three-month maternity leave went by fast. My mom helped us around the house and took care of the children while I continued my teaching assignment.

A few years later, I had the opportunity to take a short summer study course in comparative education at Harvard University. The absence of my husband, my three children, and my mother was so difficult for me while I was going to school. On the other hand, education had always been a part of my life and I took every educational opportunity that came my way.

Trip to Asia

Part of my study, was a month tour of Asia—Hong Kong, Taiwan, Japan, and the Philippines. We observed the similarities and differences in their educational systems as compared to the United States. The opportunity to travel back to my country, the Philippines, for the first time since I had moved to America was so exciting and heartwarming. It was as if an original thread of my life was being rewoven back into a broader, more beautiful tapestry.

During my visit to the Philippines, I visited my father in the cinder block house that I had bought for them in Sapang Palay, Bulacan, north of Manila. My parents had chosen a location where they felt most comfortable—an environment where people lived in simple, modest dwellings, similar to our old neighborhood. I took a jeepney to my parents' two-bedroom house, shaded by avocado, guava and mango trees. Everything looked so different. I didn't recognize anybody around me, except my father and my younger brother, Tino, who was starting to get gray hair.

With tangled emotions, I realized for the first time the impact of the sacrifices both of my parents had made for me. My mother was in America taking care of my three children while my father was living alone in his dark, gloomy, and dirty house. The house didn't seem the same. The house was in disarray. Until I saw his worn and tired face, I hadn't grasped the extent of his love and dependence on my mother. She had taken care of him for so many, many years that he didn't know where the salt and pepper shakers were kept in. By the time of my visit, she had been gone for two years helping my family with our needs in the United States.

> **True giving is letting others have what you treasure.** Francisco Samson

My brother, Tino, his wife, and our other relatives took turns cleaning, cooking and shopping for my father. Nonetheless, his health was clearly failing and he missed the comfort and care of my mother. At that moment, I grasped the difficulty of the choice my mother had made in leaving my father, just to be able to help take care of my own family. Not until then, did I understand and realize the extent of the sacrifices they had both made for me.

After being absent for a month, coming home to my own family was a joyous and loving occasion. My family was so excited and jumping with joy as they told me about their busy schedules during my absence. My husband had received a promotion, my daughters were ready to begin school, and Edward had just turned three. My mother had taught everyone some Tagalog words and phrases. It was good to come back home to the Pacific Northwest with the cool rain, the green trees, and the warmth of their love. My responsibility to my job and my students, at that moment, was the last thing on my mind.

> **Home is where your heart will always be.**

After my summer studies and my trip to Asia, I returned back to my regular teaching assignment at Queen Anne High School. Most of the students in my business classes were ambitious, and they sought a high level of accomplishment in their studies. However, some had difficulty coping and fitting in with a circle of friends. Some students had behavioral problems, which made it hard for other students to be around them. I tried to help some of the troubled students to identify their own strengths, and I talked to them about their role in taking accountability for their own actions.

One such student, Victor, had frequently fought with others outside my classroom. I had noticed his strong personality, but also his natural leadership abilities. With his parents' support, I encouraged him to run for president of the Future Business Leaders of America (FBLA), our business club, of which I was the adviser. The club overwhelmingly voted for him. They knew he could lead the club to victory. Through his leadership, our club was awarded honors in human relations and salesmanship in statewide competitions. When he had learned to focus his attention on helping other students to reach their potentials, only then did he discover his own talents and strengths. He found himself.

At this time, I also taught part-time keyboarding classes in the evening at Lake Washington Technical College. The computer had just been newly introduced in the college as a new business tool.

The following year, Queen Anne High School closed its doors permanently due to budget cut backs. The same school year, I was offered to teach full-time at Lake Washington Technical College. I taught keyboarding; word processing, beginning computer classes, and a year later, the executive secretary class. I had always enjoyed helping students overcome their anxiety about using a computer. I kept reminding them that the computer can be a friendly tool; it was nothing to worry about, and it was only as good as the peson operating it. There, I continued my longtime tradition of reading passages, and reflective, and inspirational sayings from my own life experiences. I loved to read uplifting quotes and encouraging words to my students. In fact, I encouraged my students to bring their own favorite quotes, which I wrote on the board or on the transparency sheets of the overhead projector. The students enjoyed our discussions, which helped them to relax and, therefore, to better assimilate and understand our discussions on computers.

An Immigrant's Story

Several of the students who enrolled at the college were immigrants. They told their painful stories about their lives that touched each of our hearts. Their experiences reminded me that, although I had become comfortable in America, and the sting of survival had subsided, it had never disappeared.

> **You will never know the real meaning of freedom unless it is taken away from you.**

Vantha, one of my students, told the class of her and her family's struggle for survival. Vantha, her husband, and her four children were refugees who had escaped from Cambodia. Together with another family of seven people, they had survived in a small boat floating on the Pacific Ocean. When she spoke about her life's journey, the whole class was moved. She described the night when thirteen of them, squeezed and crowded together like sardines into a small wooden boat to escape and to start a new life anywhere, except their own country. In the darkness of the night, the men quietly paddled away from the shore, unnoticed by the Cambodian police, who would have killed them, if they had seen them. They left their homeland with little food and water and just the clothes they were wearing. They feared for their lives. They had paid all the money they had, in return for their freedom. They had drifted in the Pacific Ocean for almost a month. Weak from the extreme exposure to the heat of the sun and the lack of food, Vantha's youngest daughter developed pneumonia and died in her arms. The twelve survivors were eventually rescued. All of them were deeply grateful to the U.S. Coast Guard, who had come to their rescue when they saw them floating in the Pacific Ocean, starving, run-down, fatigued, and cold. They were so thankful for the compassion of the American people.

She enrolled in my keyboarding class to improve her life, and I felt honored to be helping her achieve her goals. Her family eventually owned a home in Kirkland, Washington. She worked as a senior lead assembler in Kirkland and her husband operated his own janitorial service. All her children helped their father in his business and attended college at night when they had grown up.

> **Dreams do not discriminate—they have neither age nor limits.**

A Remarkable Dream of a Remarkable Man

As a business owner, consultant and teacher, I had the privilege of working with a broad spectrum of top corporate executives and CEO's. A common thread connecting these diverse students in excellence was a mixture of imagination, discipline, and the ability to remain flexible and focused when challenged. I soon met a mother whose son demonstrated these qualities a thousand fold. Mary and I met in several occasions at the University of Washington. I told her that her faith in his son's dream will someday come true.

This remarkable young man had a dream of changing the world of computers. We discussed how age; size, sex, or color of the skin should never be a hindrance for a dream to be realized. Him and his friend and classmate dedicated and spent hard and long hours to accomplish this dream.

As a teacher, I learn a lot from my students' mistakes. This young man had had his own share of challenges. As a teenager, his greatest drawback was his youthful appearance and his age. The computer giants did not give him a chance. He could have given up his dream; but he didn't. He persisted and continued on. This young man had a clear vision for the future. He was so focused on his dream. He was so persistent on his dream that he made the challenges and obstacles he endured into stepping stones to succeed. I had a unique opportunity to know his mother, and so I watched him grow. His parents were worried about him not completing college. He told his parents that he had just taken a "leave of absence". I was inspired by him. He persisted. I validated his plans and the magnitude of his dream in my classes. My best lesson plan was to watch him realize his dream and to let the momentum of his idea evolve. His hard work paid off. The world finally listened. His dream of having a micro-computer in every desk came true. This young man finally got heard and became the riches man in the world. I am glad to be a part of the micro-computer world. The whole universe is now benefiting from his dream. He has changed each and every one of us and has made our world a better place to live in. His name is Bill Gates.

Family Fun

Multiple job responsibilities, activities with my husband and my children, my church, and my friends filled my life with very little time for me. In the summer, we packed our belongings for a vacation to our favorite camping area. We went boating and fishing with the children and spent a month there during his and my vacation in July. We stayed at Port Susan in Tulalip, Washington.

My mother was always included on our trips. Each time she stepped on the boat, she shook her head and clicked her tongue in disbelief. She called our small fishing boat a *barco*, meaning a large ship, like the cargo ships my father used to work on. The children would fish in the deep waters of Port Susan and their faces would brighten with excitement when they would catch a bright yellow perch that glistened and flipped at the end of their fishing line. In Tagalog, my mother would praise their catches, saying what a delicious meal they had provided for our family.

Life without Mom

She also traveled with us on our long summer vacations. We visited Yellowstone National Park, Disneyland, and the Mount Rushmore National Monument. She was often over-whelmed by what she saw, and reacted by looking down toward the children and gathering them close to her for com-fort, like a hen collecting her brood. With love, she quietly and efficiently attended to our family's needs. She helped for six years. She helped the days of our busy lives to flow seamlessly.

During this time, we had received word that my father's health was declining. He needed my mother's love and attention, and we encouraged her to move back home to the Philippines to be reunited with him. After she left, the pain of her absence was enormous. Yet, the pain she must have felt by leaving my father to help us, was perhaps even greater.

Mom, the kids, and Ning on vacation

The children missed their Lola (grandmother) every day, but they adjusted to their busy school activities and sports. Maria had learned to read at the age of three, and by ten she was completely absorbed in the world of books. Juliann, at nine, showed her personal gifts in art that was reflected through her vivid drawings and portrais of her friends. Some of her artwork was used as a part of the school district's calendar. I went with her as a chaperone when she won a *Seventeen* magazine contest and was sent to New York for a week with all expenses paid. In addition, Maria and Juliann became ski instructors during the winter.

At the young age of five, Edward played T-ball with a focus and a deep desire to be a professional ball player. As he matured, his teams often became all-star baseball teams.

In the meantime, besides my full-time teaching job at the college, I taught part-time in the evening at the same campus, and had started my own business, On the JobTraining Services, which placed many of my students in jobs in the Pacific Northwest.

An Emotional Storm

During this busy time where I was fulfilling my childhood dreams, an emotional storm was building up. This new challenge was more surprising than the tornado that had flattened the campus in Xenia, Ohio, and more devastating to me than the swirling typhoon waters that had filled our home in Manila.

I was in the middle of a lecture at Lake Washington Technical College, when a courier from an attorney's office served me with divorce papers. I stood in front of my students feeling vulnerable, confused and embarrassed. This moment was also difficult for my students, as they knew that something very serious had happened. Class that day ended in a haze of confusion, but my students gathered around me with their helping hands and with their comforting words, reassuring me that everything would turn out for the best.

Change and loss had been odd companions throughout my entire life. Once again, they struck like a venomous snake's bite, to challenge me with events completely beyond my control. I immediately remembered my father's warning to me about "divorce in America," and our assurance to him that we would never get a divorce. It would bring shame to the whole family. I was too humiliated and ashamed to write my parents, to tell them that their worst fears had come true. The pain of the divorce was deepened and complicated by my culture and my Catholic faith which does not condone the disso-lution of marriage. I felt trapped by the promise that I had made to my father, and stunned by the dreadful surprise.

After sixteen years of marriage, what I thought was an ideal union was dissolved under life's unpredictable changes. The pain felt like a hot ember burning from my heart down to the soles of my feet, destroying everything in its path. My dreams for our future as a "traditional family" were crushed into pieces.

I didn't know how to approach and tell our children. First, I had to readjust to the reality of being a single mother, coping with the challenges of a new family life outside the secure framework of marriage. I couldn't explain the changes to my children because it was beyond my own comprehension. The only simple truth that my husband and I agreed on during this difficult time of our lives was to reassure our three chil-dren that we loved each one of them. It was not their fault that our marriage had ended.

I knew that my intense work ethics, which was essential to me and which had uplifted me from poverty, had contributed to the divorce. I was overwhelmed by this realization, and I struggled to understand the reason for this ironic lesson. Through spiritual counsel, I was reminded that forgiveness was the first step toward healing. I searched deeply in my own heart to forgive myself for the guilt and anger that I had turned inward. I had to learn to forgive myself before I could forgive my husband. My only strength was found in my prayers and in the loving support of my church, loyal family, friends, and neighbors, especially Lucille King, my very best friend who supported me spiritually. She was the only friend who saw me cry. I surrendered my life and faith to God's plan, wherever it might lead me, on this winding path. In this way, I hoped to find some peace to share with my children. I hope, that someday that I could be of help to other families who are also going through separation. By then, I would have a fuller knowledge and a deeper understanding and compassion for them.

> **We have to forgive ourselves before we can forgive others.**

As a married couple, my husband and I had worked together to achieve financial stability. But in the process of the divorce, I discovered that I had absolutely no financial credit to begin the life of a single mother. I didn't use credit cards; therefore, I found myself in an ironic predicament for a teacher who had taught business classes. I had to reestablish my credit all over again. I found out the hard way—a woman should have a credit of her own.

After a few years of difficult emotional and financial readjustments, I began to enjoy a renewed sense of composure and confidence. A pleasant freedom developed when personal balance was restored in my life. The children had adjusted to shared custody, and they learned to accept having a home in two separate locations. As always, Maria, Juliann and Edward were loved and cared for by both of us.

> **Forgiveness overcomes failure.**

Not By Choice

Ning Samson

Happy I was the day I took a vow

To the man I loved who stood by me somehow

"Till death do us part" is the line I will always cherish

Sixteen wonderful years for this dream come true to perish.

Our marriage was a storybook come true,

We started a family: Maria, Juliann, and, Edward, too,

Three beautiful children, our gifts from heaven above,

Are the most precious gifts and our utmost rewards.

I felt alone for the first time in my life,

The life we'd built together had now fallen apart.

I don't know what went wrong, each night I cried and trem-

bled,

The future we built together had now fallen and crumbled.

Our life hasn't really ended, it's only just begun.

We have our children to live for, to love them as I sang,

We have to make the most of what was left behind,

Look forward to an open door, and have an open mind.

This chapter of my life has ended, it is true,

My children have grown up now, and life must continue.

The lesson I have learned from this story I now voice:

Stay strong and keep the faith—God knows it was *not by*

choice.

Chapter 10

THE ULTIMATE CHALLENGE

Lesson Ten: We only succeed when we overcome our own adversities.

$\mathcal{M}$y life had tested me in many difficult ways, which always made me appreciate my mother's strength and resilience even more. She reminded me of a palm and a bamboo tree, which bend to a breaking point during a typhoon; but, then straightened again to face another storm. I had had many occasions to watch my mother's response to fear and disappointment. When the floodwaters subsided and the inside of our house was coated with a slimy layer of mud, she sang and prayed as a means of letting go of her fears and disappointments. I wanted to be more like her, and I hoped to find the strength to sing when faced with trials and conflicts

> **Experience is a hard teacher because she gives the test first, the lesson afterward.** Chinese proverb

An Unforgettable Ordeal

A few years after the divorce, God gave me another test of faith and resilience. I received a telephone call from my doctor with the results of a biopsy. I had been diagnosed with uterine cancer. I cried, and worried about my children and any hope for my future. I felt like giving up. I decided to return home to the Philippines to be in the steady, comforting care of my mother. I needed to hear her voice telling me that everything would be fine, as she would always say. I can't wait to come home. I had made arrangements for my teenage children to stay with their father while I traveled to my homeland. I had to consider major life-changing decisions for an unclear future.

Coming home to the Philippines was somewhat bittersweet due to my cancer. On the other hand, I was so happy to see my whole family together for the first time in seventeen years. They pulled up to the curb at the airport in a jeepney, which was painted brightly with swirls, stars and tropical birds, and filled with relatives. We all tearfully embraced each other. After all the welcoming and hugging, we then began the bumpy two-hour journey ride from the airport to my parent's house in Bulacan, a province north of Manila. Tino, my younger brother, carried my luggage into the bedroom in their white cinderblock house. I hugged my father and crawled into bed with my mother in the other bedroom. My body was tired, heavy with grief, and I fell asleep in my mother's arms.

> **Life is like an ocean tide—failures are the low tides, successes are the high tides, and the calmness of the sea is our peace and tranquility.**

The next day, my mother and I talked through several of my fears. She said, with the same assurance she had given me as a child that, I was going to be all right. She said that I was lucky that I had two feet to stand on and eyes to see with. She was very confident that after a long month of treatment with countless natural herbal remedies, I would be healed. This healing process, she said had been passed on to her by generations of relatives and close friends of the family. We talked constantly, day and night, to catch up on so many life events.

My mind became preoccupied with stories of the births and deaths, and successes and failures of all our friends and family.

I was so happy, and I was singing with joy to see my father again. He had sacrificed years of his life without my mother, for my own convenience. The time he had spent without her could never be repaid. When we saw each other, we cried and hugged. His eyes filled with tears behind his thick-lens eyeglasses. That was the very first time that I saw my father cry. I had noticed his black hair had turned peppered silver, and he walked slowly as he took me on a short tour of their simple home. He proudly pointed out the flushing toilet and tile bathroom, which we never had before. I told him stories about his three grandchildren, Maria, Juliann, and Edward whom he had never met, but just seen in the pictures my mother had shown him. I told him that they were getting so active. Throughout the many stories we told each other, not once did he mention anything about my divorce directly, but he said, "It's important to look forward to the future and to forget the past." At that point, I knew that he had forgiven me.

Mother's Garden

Mother showed me her garden, in an array of orange, red, and blues, exquisitely dappled in sunlight and shadow, planted next to a mango tree. I stood quietly, and admired its beauty and thought of the tiny eight-inch mound of dirt she had transformed into a garden brimming with vegetables and flowers, outside our crawl space, in downtown Manila. Her garden now was filled with orchids in every hue, color, shape and pattern. To hold the moisture in the hot climate, each orchid was planted separately in a rough, round coconut husk, which gave a creative distinction to the garden. Each sturdy spray of flowers showed brilliance in the sun, standing strong and colorful, like my mother's unrelenting spirit and welcoming smile.

Like a seed, love grows deeper as it matures.

The Cure

Both my mother and my father refused to accept the diagnosis of cancer. I don't think they even understand the complexity of the disease, much less what it does to our body. To them, it was just an infection that would heal.

My mother put me on a strict regimen of natural remedies based on teas she had made from freshly harvested herbs, tree barks, roots and leaves. She combined purple and yellow yams with tamarind and guava leaves and boiled them in a pot of water until it turned dark in color. I drank it like a tea. Another treatment was a mixture of bark from the guava tree, scraped and mixed with bittersweet melons. These, too, were boiled together to make a broth. These bitter potions were taken alternately for two weeks.

I will never forget these phases of her regimen. As soon as I drank the broth, my body began to sweat and I felt like throwing up. After a few days of drinking the brew, three to four times a day, I got use to its sharp, bitter taste. The last stage of her home treatment was a mixture of onions, garlic, tomatoes and ginger mixed into a paste-like substance that was served over rice.

My mother was so positive and reassuring that she gave me no choice but to believe in her cure. She was so sure that I would recover from this deadly disease. To me, her confidence was the most potent medicine of all. Above all, she reminded me of her faith that the strength of a woman who has suffered and survived extraordinary and unexpected turns in life was in God's hands. With this in mind, there was absolutely no reason to worry.

> **Love always heals.**

I returned to Washington after a month's visit with my parents, although I had wanted to stay longer. I felt very calm and was mentally prepared to face the doctor's recommended chemotherapy. I could hear my mother's voice telling me over and over again that I will be fine and that God was with me all the way and not to worry.

After coming back from my long trip, I went to see my doctor again. I was confident that everything was going to be fine, just like what my mother had said. As I was seated in the waiting room, I started praying the rosary holding each bead with my sweaty hands folded together. Like a child, I wanted my mother to be around. I was called in by the nurse, and I walked quietly towards a vacant room. I sat down in the examination room and prayed once again that everything would be all right. When my doctor came to check me, he ordered an X-ray to determine the size, pinpoint the exact location of the cancer, and see how far the tumor had spread. I waited for almost half an hour; but the wait seemed like forever. My doctor finally came back to the examination room and showed me the negatives reflecting through the fluorescent frame. He pointed out that there was nothing he could find; there was no cancer or tumor anywhere in my uterus. The doctor was surprised, although I was not with the results of the X-ray. He then proceeded to tell me and make me aware that the cancer must have gone into remission, which was his only logical explanation in my case. I didn't mention my trip to the Philippines, nor my mother's herbal and natural treatments. I left the doctor's office so happy, with tears in my eyes and I thanked God for another miracle. I just wished my mother had been there so I could tell her that her love and faith in God was so strong, it worked.

> **There is no better place on earth to come to than a loving home.**

After I came home from my doctor's appointment, I gathered my three children, Maria, Juliann, and Edward. I held them close to me and hugged each one with a new and deepened appreciation of how much they meant to me. I believed what my mom said, "They are your joy and purpose in life." I could not have made it without them. I never told the three of them about my cancer. I figured that, they had enough on their minds adjusting to the divorce that they didn't need to hear about the cancer. All they knew was that I looked happy, revived, smiling and very much alive after my visit with my family in the Philippines.

We went on vacation the following summer to the Oregon coast to celebrate. Yes, to celebrate life, once more. My faith in God became stronger each day. I changed my work habits. Saturdays were reserved for my children. I began to realize that life is so fragile and that I had only one life to live and I had better enjoy each moment to the fullest. My children and I enjoyed going to movies. We attended Edward's baseball games and had dinner at McDonald's afterwards. We were all grateful that our lives were back to normal. I was glad to be home in Kirkland, where the homes nestled into the hills among the maple, and fir trees, edged by the deep blue channels and bays of the Puget Sound.

After a long three-month vacation and absence from teaching, I welcomed the return of my students at the Lake Washington Technical College. I was pleased when most of my hard working, positive, and motivated students had been accepted in jobs and had gone on with their new lives as well.

The Sublime Miracle

Several years had gone by. My life was back on track. I started Business Ventures International, an import, and export trading business all over the world. My life was going well. I worked hard and still kept my teaching job. I started taking good care of myself. I ate right, exercised, and meditated each day before I taught. My children were doing well in school.

During this time, on one beautiful day in September, 1990, life presented me with another unexpected event. My morning routine was running smoothly and I had left my home to drive to my office in Redmond, Washington. Before I reached my office building, something occurred that suddenly changed my life forever. I was in my car at a stop light when another car suddenly slammed into my vehicle from behind at a high rate of speed. My vehicle was propelled across the road directly into the path of oncoming traffic where it was hit again, head-on.

My physical survival was entirely in God's hands. The impact from my car being struck from behind and hurled into a head-on collision left me immobilized. I couldn't move my arms or legs, or even move my mouth to speak; but somehow I was filled with a strong sense of peace. I remember that a bright light seemed to burst forth from the center of my body and surround the entire scene. I had the sensation of floating above my body in a state of tranquility, and I watched the ambulance attendants as they strapped me into a gurney below. The police surrounded my crushed car. In Tagalog, my birth name, Luningning, means, "shining star." At that moment, I felt that my body had turned into a star that was filled with light, with God's infinite love.

As I was rushed to the hospital, the balance between consciousness and unconsciousness was delicate, but I was filled with the undeniable calming presence of God. My life shifted into the rapid shuffle of memories that occurs, I am told, when people are dying.

In the emergency room of the hospital, my body was paralyzed. However, my mind was very much aware of the surroundings, including a staff person's discouraging remarks about my condition. Only then did I realize the complexities and the grave effects of the accident.

"She might not make it—and if she does, it's unlikely that she'll ever walk again." These doubtful words spoken at a vulnerable time triggered a fighting spirit inside me.

> **Pain is necessary before healing can start.**

Lying on the gurney in the emergency room, my mind raced with memories, like a film in fast-forward. I was fading in and out of consciousness, but I was aware enough to recall other challenging times when I had refused to give up.

One particular event in my childhood reminded me of my will to engage in a fight; to fight for what is right. I remembered protecting a friend who was being bullied by an older boy. The bully was considerably bigger and older than either of us. I tried to reason with him. When talking to him failed to defuse and resolve the calling of names, I flew uncontrollably into the boy's face with my fists, screaming and punching him as we rolled into a ditch filled with mud, broken glass and sharp tin cans. I emerged covered in mud and bleeding from cuts from the edges of the glass and metal. However, after all was said and done, he never bothered us again.

To survive the car accident, I had to call deeply and directly to that same fierce dragon in me to rise up with every ounce of my strength. But this time my fists were poised and ready to defend my own life. I was absolutely unwilling to give up. I wanted to live.

> **Never give up the will to live. One life is all we have. Embrace it.**

I was in a coma for eighteen days. A Catholic priest visited me each day, held my hand, and prayed for me. On the eighteenth day, the priest came and delivered the last rites. The attending physician made a final attempt to discern if there was any trace of life in my body. My doctor leaned close to my ear and said, "Ning, if you can hear me, try to give me any sign. Squeeze my hand."I tried to communicate to the doctor by squeezing his hand, but my body felt like a heavy steel box that walled off my ability to scream out that I was aware, and very much alive. A miracle happened, once more. My doctor managed to feel a slight movement of my hand and quickly, in a loud voice said, "She is alive. She is not dead."Once more, my prayers were heard and answered. I remember the priest praying and thanking God that I had been spared. I was alive.

Weeks later, I regained consciousness and found myself in the hospital's intensive care unit with Traumatic Brain Injury (TBI). Ironically, my brain injury was similar to the head injury my father had sustained in the motor scooter accident many years ago in Manila. When I opened my eyes, I saw that my body was connected through a network of plastic tubing to several beeping life-sustaining machines that were keeping me alive. I was frightened and confused as I tried to reorient myself, searching for anything that looked familiar and comforting. The compassionate nurse recognized the panic in my eyes. She comforted me and held my hand, while slowly and kindly explaining what had happened.

> **We have to go through our own pain before we can have a breakthrough.**

The brain and neck injury I sustained had affected my speech and the movement of my arms and right leg. My limbs were numb, I could not move and I felt trapped. I silently began to pray. My prayer was short and simple. I asked God for another chance at life so I might live to tell my story. I quietly told myself, that life is like reading a book. I need to finish each chapter to be able to grasp and understand the lessons that had to be learned from it.

I wanted to fully recover. I wanted to be able to see my children again. I wanted to watch them turn into a nice young adults. I wanted to be able to see them graduate, to watch them grow, to take care of and hug them, and to hear them say again, "I love you, too, Mom."

My simple goals strengthened my courage to survive months of painful physical therapy and rehabilitation. It tested my new level of patience and perseverance through months of speech, physical, and emotional therapy. I thank God for every breath I took.

> Patience is like a test that we must pass each time before we can advance to the next level.

My disability had forced me to be a student again in many ways. I never expected this to happen. I had to re-learn how to speak in right sequences again. I was determined. My nurses and therapists had helped a lot along the way. My hands were stiff, as though bound in cardboard and cloth, just as they had been as a child. The muscles in my fingers had to be re-trained to grasp a pencil for writing. Months and years of rehabilitation seemed endless as I struggled to retrain my leg muscles to hold the weight of my body again and again. I couldn't walk without collapsing from the pain.

My life, which had unfolded and broadened over the years, suddenly had collapsed into a small, dark space, again. I felt trapped within my body. I had to start all over again. This was another test. I talked to God and vowed to use my suffering to help and encourage others who were going through a similar crisis. In this way, my teaching took an unexpected turn from standing in a classroom into using my life experiences as a textbook.

> **Life's challenges are like hurricanes. We never know when one will strike and what surprising effects it will have on our lives.**

I remembered my father's struggle with depression after his head injury, where he recovered in small fractions of improvement. Just as my father had relied on the kindness of relatives, friends and neighbors to help him, I relied on the grace of others to help me. The accident had taught me about the loving support and kindness that is abundant in the human heart. It kept my spirit alive and well while I was recovering.

The accident depleted all my savings. The medical and hospital bills left me with practically nothing. I lost my house, went on welfare, and completely dependent upon others for support.

I eventually recovered, but I found that the accident impaired my ability to think quickly and respond to the demands of teaching. Teaching in the classroom is my first love, but I had chosen to teach in another way.

I write poetry and books of love, faith, friendship and gratitude for having been given another chance to live. I walk with joy. I am able to share the peaceful feeling in my heart with others to let them know that I would be around to help them in any way I can. I volunteer in a lot of ways and I serve the poor and the disadvantaged along the way. I hope someday that my friends and all the people I came to know would be able to share each other's Life's Long Journey.

Now, as I work in my Zen and meditative garden in my home on the Oregon Coast, I watched and enjoy the roaring blue waves of the Pacific Ocean. As I sit in my garden listening to the chirping blue jays, enjoying the soothing cold breeze blowing through my long black hair and watching the tide come and go, I often think about my own Life's Long Journey. It reminds me that life is a magnificent gift that must be rejoiced. Although many lives contain unexpected challenges, they can also be filled with love, hope, peace, and plenty of miracles..

Because I have struggled with physical and other limitations and infirmities, I have realized the importance and the true meaning of life. Writing about my experiences has served to remind myself and others with similar limitations, about the most essential lessons in life. It is very important that we embrace and remain close to our family, friends, and loved ones. Don't be afraid to share each moment of love, peace, and joy with each other. Finally, keep the hope and faith in celebrating your own Life's Long Journey.

Life's Long Journey

Ning Samson

Each passing day was a challenge

From the very early start,

The road less traveled that I chose,

My parents played an important part.

They instill the character and values

I needed to face my problems through,

They watched me climb the rugged mountains,

They hoped and prayed for my breakthrough.

Yes, one day it all happened,

All my hard work paved the way,

My life's long dream of being a teacher

And all God's blessings came my way.

Now, that I was spared to tell my story

Of my Life's Long Journey to the world,

I hope I made a difference

He gives me strength to spread His Word!

> God will never leave you nor forsake you. Focus your life in Him, and you will never go astray.

Ning today

LIST OF LESSONS, QUOTATIONS AND VERSES IN LIFE'S LONG JOURNEY

Chapter 1: Challenges from the Start

<u>Lesson One: Be thankful for what you have and make the most of what you've got.</u>

1. The effect of life's problems can either tear you apart like a hurricane or toughen you like a rock.

2. A home is a place dirty enough to enjoy and clean enough to be healthy.

3. Ask in silence. In due time, you will be answered.

4. Music uplifts the spirit. It eases away the pain in life.

5. Pray about everything and fear nothing.

6. Endure the pain and be patient. Your rewards will come sooner that you think.

7. A mother's tender and loving care overcomes any pain.

8.   Billion stars are more visible in the dark.

Chapter 2: Fight for Survival

<u>Lesson Two: Hope is present even in the most difficult circumstances</u>.

1.   In the midst of every difficulty, lies an opportunity.—Albert Einstein

2.   True giving is letting go of the things you cherished the most.—Francisco Samson, my father

3.   If everybody in town donates a thread, the poor man has a shirt.—African proverb

4.   Hunger makes hard beans sweet.—Italian proverb

5.   The more we give, the more we will receive.—Francisco Samson

6.   Adversities open doors to opportunities.

Chapter 3: A Breakthrough

<u>Lesson Three: Keep your joy in the midst of all your sorrows.</u>

1.   Miracle happens when you least expect it.

2.   Little by little, one walks far.—Peruvian proverb

3. The greatest value of the gift of knowledge is to share it to help others.—Agripina Samson, my mother

4. Education is of no value unless shared and used for the good of mankind.

5. If teaching is your calling, do it with passion.

6. To celebrate life is to celebrate the birth of Jesus.

7. Make someone happy. It will uplift your spirit; you will feel better and be rewarded in the process.

8. A creative mind can take you outside the realm of the universe.

Chapter 4: The Turning Point

Lesson Four: We only grow when we are challenged.

1. The pain of the little finger is felt by the whole body.—Tagalog proverb

2. Sing your troubles away. Music is free medicine.—Agripina Samson

3. Your struggles in life are short-lived, but your joy is long-lived.

4. Each challenge has its own corresponding lesson.

5. We can only reach the top of any mountain if we are willing to climb.

6. Often times, we know who we are, but not what we may become.

7. To be humble is to show your real self to God.

8. Don't forget to look back to where you came from or you will never reach your final destination.—Agripina Samson

Chapter 5: The Harvest

<u>Lesson Five: It is possible to live your dream. Dream the impossible.</u>

1. We can do no great things, only small things with great love.—Mother Teresa

2. To prosper is to plan, to take action, and to stay positive.

3. A gift that counts is the gift that comes from the heart.—Francisco Samson

4. The only way to discover the limits of the possible is to go beyond them—into the impossible.—Arthur C. Clark

5. Live for the moment. Don't dwell on yesterday's sorrows; instead, thank God for all his blessings.—Agripina Samson

6. I dreamed a thousand new paths; I awoke and walked my old one.—Chinese proverb

7. Today's dream can become tomorrow's reality.

8. Education can be a solid foundation for fulfilling your dreams.

Chapter 6: Change for the Better

Lesson Six: Change is a good sign of progress.

1. We cannot hold a lantern to light another's life without brightening our own.—Chinese proverb

2. Food leaves a good impression of ones love and hospitality.

3. Wisdom is learning from your own mistakes.

4. To live freely is to endure some sacrifices.

Chapter 7: Life in America

Lesson Seven: Be grateful for all that life has to offer.

1.   Share what you have gained from your life's journey so that others may learn from it.

2.   The true test of love is how much we are willing to sacrifice for each other.

3.   Have patience. Success is a process of trial and error.

4.   God's blessings are always present in the garden.

5.   Joy shared with loved ones will always be cherished.

6.   To teach is to extend your given gifts in the presence of God.

7.   Nobody is perfect. Think of the many possibilities compared to the few impossibilities.

8.   More grows in the garden than the gardener sows.— Spanish proverb

9.   There is no greater sacrifice than a mother's love for her child.

Chapter 8: A Teacher's Dream

<u>Lesson Eight: You will become what you believe.</u>

1. A child's life is like a piece of paper on which every person leaves a mark.—Chinese proverb

2. To teach is to be compassionate.

3. Education can be an important tool for changing the world around us.

4. Don't let the past poison your future. Let your setbacks be stepping stones for tomorrow's challenges.

5. Every success starts with a dream. Take a hold of it. It will someday come true.

6. Teachers open the door, but you must enter through it yourself.—Chinese proverb

Chapter 9: Trials in Life

<u>Lesson Nine: Life is filled with unexpected turns. We have to follow the winding roads before we can make a breakthrough.</u>

1. True giving is letting others have what you treasure.—Francisco Samson

2. Home is where your heart will always be.

3. You will never know the real meaning of freedom unless it is taken away from you.

4. Dreams do not discriminate—they have neither age nor limits.

5. We have to forgive ourselves before we can forgive others.

6. Forgiveness overcomes failures.

Chapter 10: The Ultimate Challenge

Lesson Ten: We only succeed when we overcome our own adversities.

1. Experience is a hard teacher because she gives the test first, then the lesson afterward.—Chinese proverb

2. Life is like an ocean tide—failures are the low tides, successes are the high tides, and the calmness of the sea is our peace and tranquility.

3. Like a seed, love grows deeper as it matures.

4. Love always heals.

5. There is no better place on earth to come to than a loving home.

6. Pain is necessary before healing can start.

7. Never give up the will to live. One life is all we have. Embrace it.

8. We have to go through our own pain before we can have a breakthrough.

9. Patience is like a test that we must pass each time before we can advance to the next level.

10. Life's challenges are like hurricanes. We never know when one will strike and what surprising effects it will have on our lives.

11. God will never leave you nor forsake you. Focus your life in Him and you will never go astray.

978-0-595-39970-3
0-595-39970-3

Printed in the United States
74583LV00003B/142-408

9 780595 399703